An Elementary Coursebook on Translation

基础翻译教程

主　编　张　焱　阮晓琴
副主编　龚　茜　杨清霜
编　者　龚　茜　胡先立　饶元锡
　　　　阮晓琴　孙安星　杨清霜
　　　　余春华　余　敏　张　焱

华中科技大学出版社
中国·武汉

内容提要

本书主要内容包括"翻译理论""翻译技巧""文体与翻译"和"中国文化翻译精选"4章。除主要章节外,本书还包含两个附加内容:"课外练习"和"翻译考试与翻译竞赛",以使学生得到更多的课外训练并了解与翻译考试和竞赛有关的信息。

本书可供非英语专业本科生使用,也可供英语专业学生及相关专业人士参考。

图书在版编目(CIP)数据

基础翻译教程/张焱,阮晓琴主编. —武汉:华中科技大学出版社,2014.8(2025.7重印)
ISBN 978-7-5609-9721-6

Ⅰ.①基⋯　Ⅱ.①张⋯　②阮⋯　Ⅲ.①英语-翻译-教材　Ⅳ.①H315.9

中国版本图书馆 CIP 数据核字(2014)第 185173 号

基础翻译教程　　　　　　　　　　　　　　　张　焱　阮晓琴　主编

策划编辑:王新华
责任编辑:王雨绵　王新华
封面设计:刘　卉
责任校对:曾　婷
责任监印:周治超
出版发行:华中科技大学出版社(中国•武汉)
　　　　　武昌喻家山　邮编:430074　电话:(027)81321913
录　　排:华中科技大学惠友文印中心
印　　刷:武汉市洪林印务有限公司
开　　本:710mm×1000mm　1/16
印　　张:9.5
字　　数:195千字
版　　次:2025年7月第1版第6次印刷
定　　价:20.00元

本书若有印装质量问题,请向出版社营销中心调换
全国免费服务热线:400-6679-118　竭诚为您服务
版权所有　侵权必究

前　言

既懂专业又具备翻译能力的复合型人才是新时代的需求,但目前这种人才十分匮乏。因此,大学英语教学已逐步重视对非英语专业学生的翻译能力的培养。同时,改革后的大学英语四、六级考试已将翻译能力纳入考查范围,翻译证书考试也吸引了大量非英语专业学生的参与。在这种形势下,许多高校为非英语专业学生开设了翻译类课程。但针对非英语专业学生的翻译教材较少,且存在一些问题:倾向于铺陈式地介绍知识和技巧,启发性不够;选材文体较单一,主要来自文学作品,不能满足当前学习和未来工作中的翻译需求;练习形式缺乏多样性。

本教材为非英语专业学生设计、编写,吸收了现有翻译教材的优点,并根据非英语专业学生的需求,着重考虑以下方面:选材的文体多样化;理论部分深入浅出,注重启发;技巧部分循序渐进;练习形式更加丰富。本教材特别设计了"中国文化翻译精选",以增强翻译的技能;介绍了"翻译考试和竞赛",为学有余力且有志于进一步学习翻译的学生提供参考。

本教材包括"翻译理论""翻译技巧""文体与翻译""中国文化翻译精选""课外练习"以及附录"翻译考试与翻译竞赛"。

"翻译理论"包含四节,分别介绍翻译的基本原理、基本方法、汉英语言的差异以及语体对翻译的要求,为学生学习翻译打下理论基础。

"翻译技巧"由八节组成,从词法到句法循序渐进地介绍和训练翻译技巧。为配合课堂教学,设计了课前活动、课堂练习和课后复习。并且在不同章节设置了"翻译赏析"等内容,方便教师选择使用,也有利于学生课后自学。

"文体与翻译"介绍不同文体的翻译原则和方法。除了学生常用到的科技文体,本教材还编写了贴近生活的"影视翻译""中国菜谱翻译"以及"标识语翻译"等版块。

"中国文化翻译精选"和附录部分的"翻译考试与翻译竞赛",能增强学生传播中国文化的能力,并为学生准备大学英语四、六级考试提供了素材。

"课外练习"部分,为学生提供大量的翻译训练材料,夯实翻译技能。

本教材的突出特点如下:

(1) 选材兼顾经典与时新、理论与技巧、知识性与趣味性;注重文体的多样性,以适应不同学生的需求。

(2) 提供导学部分和讨论部分,以练带讲,不悱不发;提供自主学习模块,注重不同层次学生的需求;除常见的翻译练习外,还设计了"跟踪阅读""佳译描红"和"翻译视听"等各种训练形式,适于合作学习和自主学习。

(3) 编排上注意线索简洁清楚,重点突出,详略得当,方便教师灵活取舍。

本书是在获得华中科技大学教务处"精品教材"立项后,由华中科技大学外国语学院基础翻译课程组老师在讲义基础上编写而成的。具体编写分工如下:龚茜编写第一章第一、二节;杨清霜编写第一章第三节;张焱编写第一章第四节,第二章第三、六、七、八节和第三章第一节以及课外练习;饶元锡编写第二章第一、二节;胡先立编写第二章第四节;余敏编写第二章第五节;余春华编写第三章第二节;阮晓琴编写第三章第三节、第四章以及附录;孙安星编写第三章第四、五节。最后由张焱和阮晓琴修改审定全书,由杨清霜校对全书。

本书得以问世,首先要感谢华中科技大学教务处和外国语学院,其次要感谢华中科技大学出版社相关编辑的鼓励与支持。英语系的王卫平老师为本书提出很多宝贵建议,在此特予以感谢。另外,还要特别感谢近几年修读"基础翻译"课程并给予反馈的同学们。

在编写过程中,编者参考了近年出版的许多相关专著、教材和期刊,详见书后的参考文献。在此,对相关作者表示感谢。由于编者水平和经验有限,书中难免会有不足之处,恳请读者批评指正,以便及时改进。

编 者
2014 年 6 月

目　录

第一章　翻译理论　/1

第一节　认识翻译Ⅰ：翻译的基本原理　/1
第二节　认识翻译Ⅱ：翻译的基本方法　/11
第三节　相遇巴别塔：汉英语比较　/17
第四节　量体裁衣：语体与翻译　/30

第二章　翻译技巧　/36

第一节　"辞严义正"Ⅰ：词义的选择和词类的转换　/36
第二节　"辞严义正"Ⅱ：词的增减　/43
第三节　挪转乾坤：翻译中的视角转换　/50
第四节　化整为零：英语长句的翻译　/57
第五节　锁定行踪：定语从句的翻译　/61
第六节　谁主沉浮：汉英翻译之"主语的选择"　/65
第七节　一一到位：汉英翻译之"谓语的处理"　/70
第八节　聚散有时：汉英翻译之"流水长句的翻译"　/76

第三章　文体与翻译　/81

第一节　严谨为先：科技翻译　/81
第二节　光影世界：影视翻译　/87
第三节　声名远播：广告翻译　/91
第四节　正确引领：标识语翻译　/97
第五节　品味中国：中国菜谱翻译　/101

第四章 中国文化翻译精选 /108

  第一节 文明传承:传统文化 /108

  第二节 文化传播:现代社会 /116

课外练习 /121

附录 翻译考试与翻译竞赛 /138

主要参考文献和网站 /141

第一章

翻译理论

第一节 认识翻译Ⅰ：翻译的基本原理

课前活动

在学习翻译之前，请从读者角度谈谈你对以下句子不同译文的看法：

(1) The dawn creeps in stealthily; when the light has become a little stronger, you have one of the fairest and softest pictures imaginable.

a. 黎明悄悄地到来。当光线变得更强一些时，你看到了能想象得到的最美好和最柔和的画面。

b. 在黎明时悄悄爬；光变得更强一点，你就有了一个最美丽的和软的图片想象。

c. 黎明悄然而至。当光线稍微变强时，一切如梦如幻，柔和淡雅，美不胜收。

(2) Both "herb" and "herbalist" are misnomers. Materials used in the aromatic but often bitter brews are not limited to the vegetable kingdom. Minerals and animal substances are also ingredients.

a. "草药"及"草药郎中"皆以讹传讹而成。这芳香四溢、苦涩难咽、救死扶伤的汤汤水水并非仅限于植物王国，矿物与动物也夹杂其间。

b. 英语里所称的"草药"及"草药郎中"，都是误称。那些略带香味但多半苦涩的汤药，其实用料并不限于植物王国，矿物和动物也常被用来配药。

(3) It may be safely assumed that, two thousand years ago, before Caesar set foot in Southern Britain, the whole country-side visible from the windows of room, in which I write, was in what is called "the state of nature".

a. 我们可以有把握地设想，两千年前，在凯撒到达不列颠南部之前，从我正在写作的这间屋子的窗户，可以看到整个原野都是处于所谓"自然状态"之中。

b. 赫胥黎独处一室之中。在英伦之南，背山而面野，槛外诸境，历历如在几下。

乃悬想两千年前,当罗马大将恺彻未到时,此间有何景物。

> 理论与实践

一、认识翻译

本章的讨论拟从翻译的定义开始。只有确立了翻译之"名",才能更好地行翻译之"实"。翻译的定义能体现人们对翻译活动的实质的看法,指明翻译活动的方向和目标。

同时,翻译活动结果的好坏,也需要有一定的"尺子"去衡量,那便是翻译的标准。建立了翻译的标准,才会有评判翻译实践好坏的"尺子"。翻译标准,不仅能提供翻译活动的规范和准则,还会使翻译活动的成果变得有意义。而这个标准的制定必须是建立在翻译定义基础上的。

那么翻译的定义是什么?翻译的标准又有哪些?

翻译的定义(definition),就其语言表述是纷繁的,但核心只有一个,即翻译是两种或多种语言之间"意义"(meaning)的转换(transform)。用"transform"这个词来比喻它是比较形象的,翻译一般被表述为转换"意义"或变形"文本"(text),即译者跨越不同的语言(前缀 trans 意味 cross),把一种语言形式的文本搬到另一种语言形式里去,而文本的内容保持不变。

换言之,翻译是把源语(the source language)表达的"意义"或"信息"用译入语(the receptor language)表达出来的语言转换行为。但这个"意义"或信息不只是存在于纯"语义"转换层面的。因此厘清这个"意义",对翻译初学者是必要的:初学者在语言转换时,往往只注意语言形式上浅表意义的转化而忽视了文化环境影响下的深层含义的移植。

人类的翻译实践证实,翻译除了语言层面即语义的转换外,还牵涉到文化层面的移植。这个现象是容易理解的,似乎简单到了呼应"语言是文化的载体"的陈述。但同时也是容易被忽视的,翻译实践中产生的大量的生搬硬套、受原文形式束缚的误译的例子,正是由没有解决语言表层形式下所隐藏的文化意义或者说遭遇到文化陷阱导致的。

现举两个例子来说明翻译中文化因素构成意义转换障碍的现象。

例如,在翻译俗语 as strong as a horse 时,翻译者既要将原短语中的深层含义"强壮"搬到汉语中去,同时也要将承载这个含义的语言浅表形式"壮如马"一并移植才行,因为唯有这样才能更好地体现出原词语的生动性。可如果原封不动地将"马"照搬到汉语中去显然是行不通的,因为汉语形容人强壮是"壮如牛"。英汉两种语言在这个形式上的差异是这两种语言赖以存在的社会文化环境不同造成的。如果硬是将"马"照搬过去,就会让国人产生一种文化上的不适应感(culture shock）；此外，译入语如果舍弃原俗语中"马"这个形象，直接将短语的深层意思表达成"强壮"的话，又会失去原短语的生动性。于是译者只得在译入语中去寻找一个类似于源语中的动物形象，且在译入语中也是用来表达"强壮"含义的，最终源语中的"马"便被替换成译入语中的"牛"了。"壮如牛"的翻译不仅照顾了汉语的表达习惯，同样也生动再现了原有的文化意象。这便是一个将意义纳入文化层面解决"如何译"的例子，有效地避免了文化差异造成意义翻译的障碍而难以被译入语读者接受的问题，同时也达到了奈达所说"译入语读者读译文的感受如同原文读者读原文的感受"之效果。同理，talk horse 也该译成"吹牛"而不是"吹马"，才不至于让译入语读者读后不知所云。

又如：英语中的"church's mouse"。其指称意义只是"教堂里的老鼠"，可深层含义却表达了"一贫如洗"的概念。如果译者在汉语中同样能找到既能体现其深层意义"一贫如洗"又能再现其源语的文化意象（"教堂里的老鼠"）的词语进行替换，就可以在译入语中产生同样生动的效果。出于这两个转换层面上的需要，"穷得叮当响"可以在译入语中再现这个短语的语义和类似的社会文化语境。虽然文化意象换成了"为数不多的几个铜币稀疏落在柜台上发出的声音"，但正是这个浅表形式上的转换生动再现了原短语中"老鼠饿了在清贫的教堂里觅食"的效果：都是用文化语境来表述贫穷，由此给两种语言的读者带来的感受也是相同的。

据此，将翻译活动的过程大致表述为：如果两种语言的语义和社会文化语境相同，翻译就可以自然转换；如果遭遇到承载语义的两种社会文化语境不同的情形，即在承载"深层含义"（内容）的源语"语言形式"（风格）和译入语的"语言形式"（风格）不同的情况下，翻译的过程便是翻译者舍弃源语中的浅表语言形式（风格），直取其源语中的深层含义（内容），再在译入语中用相似的浅表语言形式表现出来，以保证其语义和风格的不变或最大限度地接近的转化过程。

根据以上的叙述，我们不难理解一个著名的翻译论断，即"翻译就是翻译'意义'"（尤金·奈达）。但这个意义绝非是纯粹的语义，而是涵盖了语义和文化风格两个方面的"意义"，即内容和形式两个方面的"意义"。在遇到两种语言文化不对等或空缺的情况下，翻译绝非易事，这恰好揭示了翻译的实质所在。

接下来，我们将讨论翻译的标准。翻译标准是评判翻译实践（译作）好坏的尺度。传统的翻译标准的灵魂是"忠实、通顺"，主要关注的还是译文如何在保持形式不变的情况下再现原文的思想内容。在奈达的翻译理论出现之前，西方翻译界基本上也是从语言形式对等的角度来评判翻译的好坏。而当代的翻译界所持的标准则呈现"动态"趋势，将文本纳入译入语文化下，更强调译文的读者感受。从"形式对等"到"动态对等"，再到"功能对等"，我们不难追踪到西方以美国为首的翻译标准的发展轨迹。

现以一个英语冷笑话的翻译为例：

Marriage is an institution where a man loses his bachelor's degree and a woman gets her master's status.

原译:婚姻是一所学院,在里面男人失去学士学位(双关语:又指"单身汉身份"),而女人得到硕士学位(双关语:又指"主人的地位")。

英文原文通过双关的修辞手法生动、幽默地表达了对婚姻的看法:结婚后,男人的地位越来越低,而女人的地位越来越高。其中几个词都有双重含义:bachelor(学士/单身汉);degree(学位/级别);master(硕士/主人)。译文通过在括号内加注的方式,将原文的用词和内容尽量完整地表达出来。读者看过后,确实也能理解英文原文的意思,但是无法像读英文文本那样忍俊不禁地会心一笑。奈达曾指出:"如果一个贴近原文的翻译没有任何意义的话,就应该作适当的改动。"所以我们根据奈达的理论将原文进行改译。

改译:婚姻是一所医学院——男生入学主修"气管炎",女生主攻"肤必治"。

从表面上看,这个译文在形式上背离了原文,如"气管炎"和"肤必治"是原文中根本没有的两个词。但这种形式上的背离,因为与中国文化切合("气管炎"跟"妻管严"谐音,而"肤必治"是一种药物的名称,跟"夫必治"谐音),而达到了跟源语对等的幽默效果。因此说后者更符合奈达的"功能对等"的标准,即:译文在译入语中产生的效果和原文读者读原文产生的效果是一样的。

最后,就翻译理论的重要性寄语初学者。自从有了翻译活动,译者就没有停止过对翻译规律的探索。随着现代语言学中的语义学、文体学、语用学、交际理论、人类学等领域被用来研究翻译学,以及对翻译学的文化进行研究,翻译就成为一个综合性学科的,我们不仅要研究翻译中的语言问题,更要研究翻译中的文化问题了。

此外,有些翻译理论本身就是行之有效的翻译方法,在翻译活动中具有很强的操作性。面对浩瀚的材料,如果译者不去掌握一定的翻译理论,实践中就会流于凌乱。反之,如果掌握了规则和方法,自觉规范实践,就能少走弯路。

了解翻译的本质后,初学者也会抛弃诸如"了解一些英语,汉语又是母语,只要拿一本字典就可以做翻译"的误解。

二、翻译的定义

1. 国内辞书和学者下的定义

"译即易,谓换易言语使相解也。"(翻译即改变,也就是转换言语使相互了解。)

——(唐)贾公彦《周礼义疏》

"把一种语言文字的意义用另一种语言文字表达出来。"根据这个定义,翻译是两种语言之间的"转换"活动,转换的内容是"意义"。 ——《辞海》

翻译是指把一种语言文字的意义转换成另一种语言文字。换言之,翻译是一种用不同的语言文字将原文作者的意思准确地再现出来的艺术。

——许建平《英汉互译》

翻译是把一种语言所表达的信息用另一种语言传达出来的过程。

——孙万彪《高级翻译教程》

2. 著名的美国语言学家、翻译家尤金·奈达关于翻译定义的两个论述

论述一 Translating consists in reproducing in the receptor language the closest natural equivalent of the source language message, first in terms of meaning and secondly in terms of style.（所谓翻译，是指在译入语中用最贴近而又自然的对等语再现源语的信息，首先在语义上，其次在文体上。）

在与 Charles R. Taber 合著的 *The Theory and Practice of Translation* 这本书里，奈达使用了"message"（信息）一词来代替"意义"，此"信息"首先表现在"语义"上，其次表现在"文体"上；译文不仅要和原文"最大限度地接近"，还要使用"自然流畅"的译入语语言。将翻译中的"意义"概括成"语义"和"文体"，明确了翻译的任务在于转换语义和转换文体风格。"意义"的具体化对翻译活动具有现实的指导作用。

论述二 Translation means translating meaning.（翻译即译意。）

奈达在其 *Sign, Sense and Translation* 一书中，将社会符号学的成果用于对翻译的研究，提出了"翻译即译意"的著名论断，并将翻译中的"意义"细化为指称意义（designative meaning）、言内意义（intra-lingual meaning）和语用意义（pragmatic meaning）。下面将这几个意义作简要的阐述：

指称意义是指词语、句子和篇章所反映的客观世界。指称意义是一种规约的意义，不因使用者的不同而改变。例如：

（1）table cloth　桌布

（2）The sun sets down in the west.

太阳从西边落下。

言内意义是指词语与其他语言成分之间相互联系所产生的意义，主要是指句子结构意义。它体现在语音、词汇、句法和篇章各层次上的修辞手法和句式上：语音层次主要包括各种音韵（如头韵、元音叠韵、和声、押韵）、格律等；词汇层次有谐音双关、一语双叙等；句法层次有组合关系、排比、倒装等；篇章则有句式的变化、段落的安排和衔接、粘连等。翻译好文本的言内意义对再现文本的语体风格和美学价值尤为重要。例如：

（1）He described the claim in alliteration fashion as a composite of fantasy, fallacy and fiction.

他用押头韵的方式把这种诉求说成是"虚幻、虚妄和虚构的混合"。

原句中用了三个单词 fantasy、fallacy 和 fiction，它们都以字母 f 开头，发音均为/f/，在英语里这叫"头韵"，通过押头韵的方式强调了"他的诉求"；汉语里没有押头韵，但变通为以同一个"虚"字开头，也传递了同样的美学效果。

(2) The senator picked up his hat and courage.

参议员捡起了帽子,也鼓起了勇气。

原文用了 pick up 去搭配两个不相干的事物,一个是具体的"帽子",另一个是抽象的"勇气",这叫"一语双叙"的修辞法。汉语将同一个动词短语 pick up 分别译成为"捡起"和"鼓起"来搭配两个不同的宾语,同时在"捡起"和"鼓起"间加个"也"字,恰好再现了原文的幽默俏皮,又照顾了汉语的措辞习惯。

(3) Read not to contradict and confute; nor to believe and take for granted; nor to find talk and discourse; but to weigh and consider.

读书时不可存心诘难作者,不可尽信书上所言,亦不可只为寻章摘句,而应推敲细思。

原文用了排比,译文也要用排比,这样很好地翻译出原文的语气和风格,既工整又起到了强调的作用。

语用意义是指语言与语言使用者之间的关系,是语言在使用过程中即在特定语境下产生的意义。语用意义必须是以指称意义为基础的。例如:

(1) You look darker after holidays.

指称意义是:度假后你晒黑了。

语用意义或许要表达:度假后你显得更健康了。

(2) 你吃饭了吗?

指称意义是:Have you eaten?

语用意义或许是:Hello!(汉语中熟人见面问"吃饭了没有"并不是真的关心吃饭没有,而是一种非正式的寒暄。)

(3) eat one's words

另外要注意指称意义和语用意义不一致所带来的翻译陷阱,不能将其翻译成"食言",而是"承认自己说错话","收回前言"的意思。

奈达将"意义"细化为指称意义、言内意义、语用意义,对于实践操作具有指导意义:翻译作品质量的好坏取决于译文能在多大程度上再现原文的三种意义及其伴随的六大功能(信息功能、表情功能、祈使功能、美感功能、酬应功能、元语言功能)。总的说来,译文再现原文的意义和功能越多,质量就越好。有时指称意义、信息功能非常突出(如科技作品),有时语用意义、言内意义及美感功能可能占有非常重要的地位(如文学性话语)。另外,源语和译入语在三种意义及各种功能方面能同时对等的情形非常少见。这就需要译者根据具体情况,在不可能把原文所承载的各种意义和功能全部传递给译入语读者的情况下,善于抓住最重要的意义和功能,将损失减少到最低的程度。

三、翻译的标准

翻译的标准既是译者在实践中需要遵循的规则和方法,也是衡量翻译质量好坏的尺度。

1. 严复的三字原则：信、达、雅

严复的贡献不仅在其翻译了 T. H. Huxley 的《天演论》、Adam Smith 的《原富》、Montesquieu 的《法意》以及 H. Spencer 的《群学肄言》等著名的西方著作，更重要的是他根据我国古代翻译佛经的经验，结合他的翻译实践，在《天演论》卷首的《译例言》中提出了"信、达、雅"翻译三字标准（Three-word Principle：faithfulness, expressiveness and elegance）。

"信"是"意义不背本文"，"达"是"不拘原文形式，尽译文语言之能事以求原意明显"。"信""达"互为照应，不可分割开来。

"雅"是指用汉代以前的词法句法来表达，由于严复师从于唐宋八大派的桐城派，他认为只有用了古文骈体的译文才够"雅"。

须批判性地接受"雅"：如果原文不雅，译文何以求雅？同时要赋予"雅"新的解释：译文要具有与原文相适应的文采。在"信达雅"的基础上，刘重德提出了"信、达、切（closeness）"，即"切合原文风格"才是真正的"信"。

2. 国内译界对翻译标准的概述：忠实（faithfulness）、通顺（smoothness）、贴切（closeness）

"忠实"，首先指忠实于原作的内容，不篡改、歪曲或任意增删原作内容。内容通常指作品中叙述的事实、说明的事理、描写的景物以及作者在叙述、说明和描写过程中所反映的思想、观点、立场和所流露的感情等。

"通顺"，指译文语言必须通顺易懂，符合译入语规范，应该是明白畅晓的现代语言，译文中没有逐词死译、硬译的现象，也没有文笔不通、结构混乱、逻辑不清的现象。

"贴切"，指翻译还应再现原作的风格，即保持原作的民族风格、时代风格、语体风格、作者个人的语言风格等。从某种意义上来讲，这也是一种"忠实"。

当然，译文的通顺度应与原文的通顺度一致。例如，在文艺作品中，作者有时有意识采用一些非规范语言以刻画人物或渲染某种气氛，翻译时就不宜片面追求"通顺"而加以改变，应尽可能把原著中一些非规范化语言也如实加以传达。当然这种情形属于特例。

3. 奈达：从"形式对等"标准到"动态对等"标准

"形式对等"指的是词与词、句与句等各种因素的对等或相当，是以源语为中心的（source-oriented），这个标准在表层形式和深层意思一致时可用。例如：

（1）blue ribbon beer　蓝带啤酒
（2）trading partners　贸易伙伴

而"动态对等"则指翻译应该是内容的传递在先，其次才是形式的传递。奈达认为文化差异决定了源语文本与译入语文本只能是相对的对等，为了考虑译文的可接受性，译者应采用变通手段，来达到译入语读者读译文和原文读者读原文一样的效果。他主张从译文接受者角度而不是从译文形式角度来看待翻译，这就是动态对等。当形式和内容发生冲突时可以舍弃原文的形式，直取其深层次的含义，然后在译入语中用基本相同的浅层次的形式表达出来。动态对等可在表层形式与深层意思不一致时用。下面通过例子来演示动态对等的翻译过程：

(1) as strong as a horse

第1步：翻译成"壮如马"——保留原文的形式"马"，但会产生类似于"cultural shock"的生硬感。

第2步：舍弃原文的形式，直取其深层含义"很壮"，但会失去原文的生动性。

第3步：在译入语中找类似于原文的表达——将深层含义重新用译文的浅表形式表达出来。

第4步：翻译为"壮如牛"。

以上4步完成了从"形式对等"到"动态对等"的转化。

(2) 歌名：*Right Here Waiting*

译为"在此等待"——形式相当

译为"此情可待"——功能相当

奈达曾将翻译表述为："Translating consists in reproducing in the receptor language the closest natural equivalent of the source language message, first in terms of meaning and secondly in terms of style."此定义中的closest和natural两词恰好表明了奈达对于翻译的态度：翻译的本质和任务是用标准的译入语再现源语信息，翻译要使用"最切近"而又"最自然"的对等语。动态对等可归纳成以下四个标准：

(1) 传达信息；

(2) 传达原作的精神风貌；

(3) 语言顺畅自然，完全符合译入语规范和习惯；

(4) 读者反应类似。

所以判断译文质量的标准最终基于三个方面：能使接受者正确理解原文信息；易于理解；形式恰当，吸引接受者。这个翻译标准打破了以往的静态标准的模式，形成了一种开放性标准，这就是奈达著名的动态对等(dynamic equivalence)或叫功能对等(functional equivalence)理论。

跟踪阅读

翻译大家谈翻译标准

(1) 释道安的"案本"，即按照原文的本意。

(2) 唐代佛经翻译家玄奘主张翻译"既须求真又须喻俗"。(A good translation should be both faithful to the original and intelligible to the public.)

(3) 傅雷的"神似"与钱钟书的"化境","神似"在于以神统形,"化境"在于有意境美。

(4) 鲁迅先生提倡:"凡是翻译,必须兼顾两面,一则当然力求其易解,一则保存着原作的丰姿。"这和译文必须忠实原文与通顺实质上是一致的。

(5) 英国翻译家乔治·坎贝尔(George Campbell)的翻译三原则:The first thing... is to give a just representation of the sense of the original... The second thing, to convey into his version, as much as possible, in a consistency with the genius of the language with which he writes, the author's spirit and manner... The third and the last thing is, to take care, the version has at least, so far the quality of an original performance, as to appear natural and easy...(首先,准确再现原作的意义;其次,在符合译作语言特征的前提下,尽可能传递作者的精神和风格;最后,译作至少具有原创作品的特性,自然流畅。)

(6) 英国翻译家泰特勒(Alexander F. Tytler)的翻译三原则:

a. The translation should give a complete transcript of the ideas of the original work.(译作应完全复写原作的思想。)

b. The style and manner of writing should be of the same character with that of the original.(译作的风格和写作手法应和原作属同一性质。)

c. The translation should have all the ease of original composition.(译作应具有原作的通顺度。)

思考与练习

1. 翻译的定义五花八门,对它们的归类可以因角度而异。根据你的阅读积累,思考对翻译定义还可以如何进行分类。
2. 请你介绍一两个令你印象最为深刻的翻译定义。
3. "Translation means translating meaning."这个命题中的"meaning"包含哪三个方面的内容?
4. 奈达的社会符号学是如何阐明翻译的实质和指出翻译的目的和任务的?试举例说明。
5. 下面是《江雪》中"千山鸟飞绝,万径人踪灭"的几种译文,谈谈译者分别是怎样兼顾"指称意义"和"言内意义"的。
   (1) O're any hills no birds are seen.
      In any paths no footprints show.(赵甄陶译)
   (2) From hill to hill no bird in flight.
      From path to path no man in sight.(许渊冲译)
   (3) A hundred mountains and no bird.

A thousand paths without a footprint. (Witter Bynner 译)

6. 译文必须做到忠实与通顺,请指出下面句子的译文不够忠实或通顺的地方并加以修改。

"Enjoyed" is too mild a word. I walked on air. I really lived.

"享受"是太温和的一个字。我行走在空气中。我真正地活着。

改译:_____

7. 你能找到一些奈达的符号学翻译法用在文学、广告、影视作品台词等翻译里的例子吗?

第二节 认识翻译Ⅱ：翻译的基本方法

课前活动

请你判断一下：以下句子的译文，哪些是直译，哪些是意译？
(1) I talked to him with brutal frankness.
a. 我同他谈话用粗暴的坦率。
b. 我同他谈话时，使用了令人不快的真诚的语言。
c. 我对他讲的话，虽然逆耳，却是忠言。
(2) His irritation could not withstand the silent beauty of the night.
a. 他的烦恼不能承受夜晚宁静的美丽。
b. 他的烦恼经不起这宁静的良宵美景的感染。
c. 面对这宁静的良宵美景，他的烦恼不禁涣然冰释了。

理论与实践

一、翻译基本方法之"直译与意译"

1. 直译与意译的定义

Literal translation strives to reproduce both the ideological content and the style of entire literary work and retain as much as possible the figures of speech and the main sentence structures or patterns.

直译指尽量完整地再现原文的思想内容和表达风格，并尽量保留原文主要的句子结构和修辞特点。

Free translation is a supplementary means to mainly convey the meaning and spirit of the original without trying to reproduce its sentence patterns or figures of speech. (Peter Newmark, 2001)

意译指在不拘于原文的句式结构和修辞特点的情况下，传达出原文的意义和风貌。

不管是直译还是意译，都应该在意义上忠实于原文，在表达上通顺晓畅。直译不是死译、硬译，意译不是乱译。

2. 辩证看待直译与意译

首先，直译和意译是相对而言的，无法对它们做绝对的区分。比如：to kill two

birds with a stone 可译为：①一石二鸟；②一箭双雕；③一举两得……一般认为①是直译，但这里多少还是有一点意译的成分，毕竟"一石二鸟"和源语相比，在用词上做了一定的省略，需要添加一些词才基本一致：（以/用）一（块）石（头）（击杀/打死……）二鸟。②③没有译出源语中的"石"和"鸟"，一般被看作意译，但数字的对应却是直译。

对于什么时候该直译，什么时候该意译也没有绝对的要求。一是要看译者的翻译目的，二是要遵循翻译的一般原则，即能直译尽量直译，不能直译就采用意译的方法。

源语与译入语在内容和形式上完全对等时，应采用直译，如：

（1）to add fuel to the fire

火上浇油

（2）一国两制。

One country, two systems.

（3）七夕节源自中国的一个古老传说。

The Qixi Festival originated from an ancient Chinese legend.

有时，源语在译入语中并没有对应的说法，但可以被译入语受众理解，甚至丰富了译入语的表达方式。此时，也可用直译的方法。如：

（1）All the world is a stage. (William Shakespeare)

世界就是一个舞台。

（2）Time is money.（英语谚语）

时间就是金钱。

但是，我们在进行语言解读转换的时候，经常会遇到由于句法结构、思维方式、审美取向的不同而造成的种种障碍，这些障碍往往难以逾越，此时，若直译不能充分传达原文的神韵，甚至佶屈聱牙、拖沓累赘、引起歧义，就应大胆地以意译为辅，甚至完全意译。试比较以下例句的不同译文：

（1）breadwinner

直译：挣面包者

意译：养家糊口之人

（2）Last year I inherited some money from my grandmother, but I haven't spent it yet. I'm saving it for the rainy days.

直译：去年我从祖母那继承了一笔钱，但没有花。我存起来以对付雨天。

意译：去年我从祖母那继承了一笔钱，但没有花。我存起来备急需之用。

（3）Nothing could be done.

直译：无事可以被做。

意译：我们无能为力。

3. 直译不等于死译，意译不等于乱译和胡译

无论用哪种翻译方法，目的都是为了达到"忠实、通顺、贴切"的翻译标准。拘泥于原文而不能变通，就变成了死译；天马行空，无中生有，与原文意义和风格相悖，就变成了乱译。以课前活动的句子为例：

I talked to him with brutal frankness.

译文一：我同他谈话用粗暴的坦率。（死译）

译文二：我同他谈话时，使用了令人不快的真诚的语言。（直译）

译文三：我对他讲的话，虽然逆耳，却是忠言。（意译）

译文四：我跟他谈话使用了凶残的语言，但一片冰心在玉壶。（乱译）

二、翻译基本方法之"归化与异化"

1. 归化与异化的定义

Domestication refers to the translation strategy in which a transparent, fluent style is adopted in order to minimize the strangeness of the foreign text for target language readers, while foreignization designates the type of translation in which a target text "deliberately breaks target conventions by retaining something of the foreignness of the original" (Shuttleworth & Cowie, 1997).

归化（domestication）的翻译方法，是指采用明晰、流畅的风格，最大限度地淡化原文的陌生感。即译者向译入语读者靠拢，尽可能地使源语文本所反映的世界接近译入语读者的世界，从而达到源语文本与译文之间的"文化对等"。

而异化（foreignization）的翻译方法，则指在一定程度上保留原文的异域性，故意打破译入语常规。它主张译者向作者靠拢，翻译时保留源语文化，译文呈现出浓厚的异国情调。

2. 归化、异化与直译、意译的区别

异化与归化和直译与意译这两组概念，既相似又有所不同。直译与意译关注的是如何在语言层面处理形式和意义，即翻译技巧运用的问题；而异化与归化的概念则侧重于文化和美学等因素的转换，即不同文化及意识形态之间的转换问题。例如：

《红楼梦》句：鸡儿吃了近年粮。

杨宪益、戴乃迭译：It's been like hens eating up next year's grain.

大卫·霍克斯译：Every month now our allowance falls short of our expenditure.

对这个句子的两个不同翻译版本，既可以从"直译"和"意译"的层面来比较，也可以用"归化"和"异化"的概念来探讨。以杨宪益、戴乃迭的译文为例，从语言层面来看，该译文更大程度地保留了原有的词汇和修辞手法，采用了更倾向于"直译"的

翻译方法。而从文化角度来看,它保留了中文的俗语,对西方读者来说,具有来自东方的"异国情调",因此采用的又是"异化"的翻译方法。

3. 处理好归化与异化的关系

归化与异化既对立又统一,相辅相成。完全归化和完全异化都不成其为翻译。所以译者往往需要采用归化和异化两种方法。至于更倾向于哪一种方法,要依具体情况而定。请看下面两个例子:

(1) High buildings and large mansions are springing up like mushrooms in Beijing.

译文一:在北京,高楼大厦犹如蘑菇般地涌现。

译文二:在北京,高楼大厦犹如雨后春笋般地涌现。

译文一按照原文译为"犹如蘑菇般",虽体现了原文的风格,但会给中国的读者带来生硬感。译文二进行归化处理,把 like mushrooms 译为"犹如雨后春笋般",符合中国的地貌风情和语言习惯。

但是,在小说《苔丝》的翻译中,译文用归化方法进行语言处理时则受到翻译评论家的质疑。

(2) "Of course it may," said Angel. "Was it not proved nineteen hundred years ago—if I may trespass upon your domain a little?"(T. Hardy: *Tess of the d'Urbervilles*, Ch. 25)

译文:"当然可以,"安琪尔说,"如果我可以班门弄斧地说一句话,这不是在一千九百年以前就被证明了的吗?"

"班门弄斧"这样的极具汉语特征的成语一般不宜用在译文当中,尽管这些成语可能更形象,但会造成文化错觉,失去源语味道。

在翻译实践中,究竟以哪种方法为主,还受译入语读者、翻译目的和文本体裁等因素的影响,如果需要保留源语中文化的意象,从而呈现异国情调,翻译中就往往更多采用异化的方法。但如果强调译作的可读性和通俗性,那就需要关照译入语读者的文化习惯,更多采用归化的翻译方法,如电影对白的翻译。

有学者指出,随着各民族之间的文化交流不断加强,文化差异性逐步减小,文化趋同性逐步提高,读者的接受心理和审美期待也发生了很大的变化。对现代文学的翻译,译者比以前更多使用异化的翻译方法,以满足读者对语言新颖性的需求。以小说 *Gone with the Wind* 的翻译为例,二十世纪四十年代傅东华先生的翻译版本更多运用了归化方法,如将主人公名字 Scarlett O. Hara 译为具有中国味道的"郝思嘉",美国名城 Atlanta 被译为带有中国地名特色的"饿狼陀"等。而二十世纪九十年代陈廷良等的翻译版本则保留了更多"洋味",如 Scarlett O. Hara 被译为"斯嘉丽·奥哈拉"。由上可见,归化与异化两种方法之间的平衡点,不是一成不变,而是动态发展的。

跟踪阅读

翻译大家谈直译和意译

茅盾:"我以为所谓'直译'也者,倒并非一定是'字对字',一个不多,一个也不少。……'直译'的意义就是不要歪曲了原作的面目,要能表达原作的精神。"(《翻译通讯》,1984b:17)

朱光潜:"所谓'直译'是指依原文的字面翻译,有一字一句就译一字一句,而且字句的次第也不改动。"(《翻译通讯》,1984b:362)

冯庆华:"所谓直译,就是既保持原文内容,又保持原文形式的翻译方法或翻译文字。……所谓意译,就是只保持原文内容、不保持原文形式的翻译方法或翻译文字。"(《实用翻译教程》)

巴金:"我觉得翻译的方法其实只有一种,并没有'直译'和'意译'的分别。好的翻译应该都是'直译',也都是'意译'。"(巴金:《一点感想》,见《翻译通报》1951年5月第2卷第5期)

思考与练习

1. 什么是直译和意译?直译和死译的区别在哪儿?意译、乱译和胡译的区别在哪?试举例说明。
2. 什么是归化与异化?归化与异化和直译与意译的相似点与不同点在哪儿?
3. 请指出电视剧《生活大爆炸》中应用的归化翻译法成功在哪儿。
4. 杨宪益、戴乃迭英文版的《红楼梦》与大卫·霍克斯版的《红楼梦》在翻译方法上有什么不同?各自的翻译目的是什么?
5. 请将以下的词组翻译成汉语,根据需要使用直译或意译的方法:
   (1) pillar industry
   (2) Wet paint!
   (3) Exporting to a certain number of countries is made difficult by the quantity of red tape.
6. 翻译时应将文化因素纳入考虑,不可望文生义。请判断以下译文中哪个才是正确的。
   (1) We parted the best friends.
   a. 我们告别了最好的朋友。
   b. 我们在分别时是极好的朋友。
   (2) That's all Greek to me.
   a. 那对我来说全是希腊语。

b. 那个我可一窍不通。

(3) He is as good as dead.

a. 他同死一样好。

b. 他几乎死掉。

(4) Do you see any green in my eye?

a. 你从我的眼睛里看到绿色吗?

b. 你以为我是好欺负的吗?

(5) Tom was upsetting the other children, so I showed him the door.

a. 汤姆一直在扰乱别的孩子,我就把他带到门那。

b. 汤姆一直在扰乱别的孩子,我就把他撵了出去。

第三节　相遇巴别塔：汉英语比较

课前活动

看看以下四组句子,你能找出英汉两种语言的哪些差异?
(1) 你有种,我要给你点颜色瞧瞧。
译文一:You have seed. I will give you some color see see.
译文二:You have guts. I will teach you a lesson.
(2) 七八个星天外,两三点雨山前。
Beyond the clouds seven or eight stars twinkle;
Before the hills two or three raindrops sparkle.
(3) 善有善报,恶有恶报。
Good is rewarded with good, and evil with evil.
(4) He never forgets to cross his t's and dot his i's.
他是个一丝不苟的人。

理论与实践

《圣经旧约·创世纪》的第十一章(Genesis 11)里记载着著名的巴别塔(The Tower of Babel,又名通天塔)的故事:很久以前,世上的人们都使用同一种语言,不存在沟通障碍。人们彼此容易沟通,也就容易齐心协力,从而变得强大起来。为了显示力量传扬声名,他们计划建造一座通天的高塔。此塔尚未建成,耶和华上帝已觉不妥:如果人们连这样宏伟的高塔都能建成,那么以后他们想做的事就无所不成。于是上帝变乱了他们的语言,沟通就成了极大的障碍,高塔自然无法完工,人们也分散到世界各地。早期圣经主要是用希伯来语记述的,在希伯来语中"巴别"是变乱的意思,所以后世又将此塔命名为巴别塔,标记着人们语言的分化。

无论是否真有其事,圣经中的这段记载都指出了语言沟通的重要性。没有语言障碍、团结一致的人们力能通天;而因语言障碍无法交流、一盘散沙般的人们只能被禁锢在大地上。从这个意义上说,学习和从事翻译的人们就是巴别塔下雄心勃勃的仰望者和实干家,他们期待用自己的努力重建沟通,进而重建高塔、开拓碧空。而这座未能完工的巴别塔带给我们的第一课便是语言的差异。

语言学家们把世界上的语言大致分为九大语系,汉语属于汉藏语系,英语属于印欧语系。同一语系内的语言较容易寻找对应关系,不同语系的语言则比较困难。

英汉两种语言分属不同语系,要在二者之间进行翻译自非易事。因此,明确英汉语言的基本差异,成为我们学习翻译的初始步骤。大略而言,汉语为象形文字,每个字由若干笔画构成,英语为拼音文字,每个词由若干字母构成;汉语有平、上、去、入四声,英语则分为升调、降调两种。不过,仅仅意识到这个大略的差异对翻译而言是远远不够的。本节将从较小的语言单位即字词短语的差异谈起,逐步扩大至句法篇章的差异,乃至文化差异,以便为这两种语言之间的转换打下基础。

一、汉英词汇对比

(1) 英语中许多单词的词性改变经常伴随着拼写的改变,比如名词 friend,对应的形容词形式是 friendly,动词形式是 befriend。而汉语的字词的词性改变时,书写是不会随之更改的。如"友风子雨"一词中"友"和"子"都是动词,表示把风当作朋友,把雨当作孩子。"扶老携幼"一词中,"老"和"幼"不是形容词而是名词,表示老人和幼儿。又如"大楚兴,陈胜王",其中"王"字也不是现代汉语中常见的名词,而是动词,表示"称王"的意思。在翻译时如果不注意词性变化就容易出错。

(2) 英语可数名词大多有单、复数形式之别(当然有少数英语名词是单、复数同形的,如 deer、sheep 等),汉语名词则没有单、复数形式的变化。"一头狮子"和"一群狮子"在汉语中名词"狮子"的书写与读音都不会发生变化,而英语中 a lion 和 a pride of lions 单、复数区别一目了然,读音也略有不同。

(3) 量词是汉语特有的一类词语,英语中没有量词一说。还是以上文"一头狮子"和"一群狮子"为例,"头"和"群"都是量词。但是英语中 a lion 便没有对应的量词。至于 pride,依旧是名词,表"兽群"之意,指若干狮子组成的兽群。

(4) 汉语和英语都有三种人称,但是当动词出现在英语的第三人称单数后面时,要做相应的改变,汉语中则没有这种动词的变化。例如:

I like reading.　我喜欢阅读。
You like reading.　你(们)喜欢阅读。
He likes reading.　他喜欢阅读。
They like reading.　他们喜欢阅读。

以上四组例句包含三种人称,其中英语动词 like 在第三人称单数 he 后面有所不同,汉语动词"喜欢"则始终如一。

(5) 汉语的时态划分比较大略,通常用时间状语(如"昨天""刚才""明年")或时态助词(如"了""过""着")表示。英语则是一种时态划分非常清晰的语言,共有十六种时态。汉语的动词不会随着时态的变化而改变,英语动词则不然。下面以其中最常见的六种英语时态为例:

He reads the book. 他在读这本书。
He read the book. 他读过这本书。
He is reading the book. 他正读着这本书。

He was reading the book. 当时他正在读这本书。

He has read the book. 他已经读过这本书了。

He had read the book. 以前他就读过这本书。

以上六组例句中,英语动词 read 的形态随时态变化而改变,汉语动词"读"则始终如一。

(6) 动宾搭配。不同的语言有不同的搭配习惯,在翻译时必须充分意识到这种习惯上的差异。如汉语动词"晒"的动宾搭配:

晒太阳　bathe / bask in the sunshine

晒被子　air the quilt in the sunshine

晒黑　get suntanned

晒工资　divulge the salary

英语动词 deliver 的动宾搭配:

deliver letters　送信

deliver a lecture　做讲座

deliver a baby　接生孩子

(7) 定语的排列和位置。当多个英语形容词作前置定语,即放在被修饰的中心词之前时,其排列顺序为"数量+描绘+规模+形状+新旧+颜色+地点+材料+性质+中心词"。而当多个汉语形容词作定语前置时,排列顺序则灵活得多。例如:

a. This is a precious huge round old red Chinese oak dining table.

可译为:这是一张颇有年头的、珍贵的红色中式巨型橡木圆餐桌。

也可译为:这是一张颇有年头的、珍贵的巨型中式红色圆形橡木餐桌。

当定语包含短语或分句时,英语中通常将分句和短语放在中心词之后;汉语中则多数将它们放在中心词之前。

b. A woman caught running an illegal bus service refuses to bribe a soldier and instead openly screams abuse and chases him off.

一名因进行非法汽车营运被捕的妇女不仅不向逮捕她的士兵行贿,反而公然大骂,把他赶走了。

c. A first-half goal from Liverpool striker Fernando Torres was enough to see off the Germans, who were outclassed by a strong Spanish side.

来自利物浦前锋费尔南多·托雷斯的一个上半场进球足以击败实力远不如西班牙队的德国队。

(8) 状语的排列。状语分为时间状语、地点状语、原因状语、方式状语等多类,在汉英两种语言中的排列顺序之不同难以一一列举,所以下面挑选最常见的几种区别进行说明。

首先,汉语中凡提及地点,一般都从最大的范围开始,逐步缩小到最具体的地方。英语恰恰相反,一般从最具体的地方开始,范围逐步扩大。比如大家商量春游活动的集合地点,会说"我们在武昌东湖公园正大门处集合吧",英语须翻译成"let's meet at the main entrance to the East Lake Park in Wuchang District"。在书写信封地址时也是如此,如"湖北省武汉市华中科技大学外国语学院"就要翻译成"School of Foreign Languages, Huazhong University of Science and Technology, Wuhan, Hubei"。

其次,汉语中习惯的因果关系的排列多数情况下是先因后果,当然也有少数例外,如强调句型"之所以……是因为……"。英语中多数情况下更习惯于先果后因的排列。

例:因为今天下雨,所以我们不能去野餐。

误译:Because it's raining today, so we can't go picnic.

更正:We can't go picnic today because it's raining.

二、汉英句法对比

1. 竹形结构与树形结构

汉英句法上的差异大体而言是竹形结构和树形结构的差别。

汉语句子好似一根竹子,框架简约;每段竹节之间的差别不是太大,即各类语法范畴比较模糊;句内成分的排列顺序也没有特别严格的规定,整句话的逻辑关系是内在的、隐性的,需要读者去意会。因此汉语被认为是"意合"的语言,这里"合"就是"连接""组合"的意思。

英语句子则像一棵大树,框架严谨;树的主干枝丫分明,即各类语法范畴比较明确;句内成分的排列顺序有相对严格的规定,整句话的逻辑关系是外在的、显性的,形式结构十分清晰。由于强调形式结构,英语也相应地被认为是"形合"的语言。以几个简单的汉语句子为例:

(1) 今天咱们吃食堂吧。

Let's go to the canteen for lunch/dinner.

以汉语为母语的人都能听懂这句话,不会产生什么歧义。但是,假如套用英语的主谓宾结构来分析一下,就会发现此句中的施动者与受动者的关系颇为奇特。食堂作为建筑物是无法充当人类食物的,只有食堂里的饭菜才可吃。所以,"吃食堂"吃的并非食堂,食堂只是进餐地点罢了。翻译成英语时就需要进行相应的调整。

(2) 人不犯我,我不犯人。

We will not attack unless we're attacked.

在汉语里,分句之间的逻辑关系可以靠读者意会,译文中要加上"unless"来明示句间关系。

(3) In the doorway lay at least twelve umbrellas of all sizes and colors.

如果译文采用原文的树形结构(主从结构),就显得比较拗口:

门口放着至少有十二把五颜六色、大小不一的伞。

译为汉语的"竹形结构",读起来就轻松多了:

门口放着一堆雨伞,少说也有十二把,五颜六色,大小不一。

2. 省略

英语句子一方面非常注重语法结构,另一方面又喜欢通过省略使行文简洁。在并列或排比的结构中,英语句子往往省略前文出现过的、相同的词语。汉语则倾向于重复这些词语,形成对称的结构。例如:

(1) 近朱者赤,近墨者黑。

Association with the good can only produce good, with the wicked, evil.

(2) Studies serve for delight, for ornament and, for ability.

读书足以怡情,足以博采,足以长才。(王佐良译)

3. 主语

根据有无生命划分,主语可分为有灵主语(animate subject)和无灵主语(inanimate subject)。常见的有灵主语是有生命的人或物,常见的无灵主语则是抽象的概念。汉语句子注重主体性叙述,多采用有灵主语,少用(并非完全不用)无灵主语;英语句子更倾向于客体性描述,比汉语更多地采用无灵主语。例如:

(1) 我在这个学校已经待了四年。

The campus has seen me for four years.

(2) This Thanks-giving morning had seen us busily preparing a traditional dinner featuring roast turkey.

那个感恩节的上午,我们在忙着准备一道以烤火鸡为主的传统菜肴。

汉语中还有一类特殊的无主句,即从语态上看句子属于主动态,可是动作的施动者并不出现。例如:

春节应该吃饺子。

"春节"作为节日是无法发出"吃"这个动作的,因此"春节"只是句中点明时间的成分而已,吃饺子的还得是人。所以翻译时应补充主语 people。该句可译为:

Traditionally people eat jiaozi during the Spring Festival.

4. 语态

汉语句子主动语态较多,并且经常用人做主语。如数学课上老师说:"我们已经知道根号2是无理数。"

英语句子被动语态较多,尤其在陈述客观事实时。数学老师说的这句话用英文表达就是:It has been known that the square root of 2 is an irrational number.

有时候,句子的主语是某人或某些人是不言而喻的,所以按照汉语习惯经常把这类主语省略掉,同时保持句子的主动语态不变,形成汉语无主句。例如若要把"现在可以得到结论了"翻译成英语,可以有如下两种处理方式:

译文一:Now we arrive at the conclusion.(保持主动语态,补充主语 we。)

译文二：Now the conclusion can be drawn.（译为被动语态,将原句的宾语作为译文的主语。）

5. 主题突出与主语突出

汉语句子常用"主题＋述题"的形式,先突出谈论的主题,再把对该主题的评论娓娓道来。例如：

这些生肖铜首,一个比一个售价高。（电影《十二生肖》）

此句先点明谈论的主题是从圆明园流失到海外的兽首铜像,然后再从售价上对它们进行评论。如翻译时不加思考,照搬汉语句式,则会出现如下译文：

These bronze heads, one is more expensive than another.（误译）

而英语句子常用的是"主语＋谓语"的形式,突出的是主语。因此该句可以改译为：

The prices of these bronze heads go higher and higher one after another.

再如,2013年网上流行迷你剧《万万没想到》中的一句台词："背黑锅,我们特专业。"此句首先展示谈论的主题是"背黑锅"这一事件,然后就此事件给出阐述"我们特专业"。从主谓角度分析,首先出现的"背黑锅"并非全句主语,紧随其后的"我们"才是。所以翻译成英语的时候需要适当调整语序：

We are professional in playing the role of scapegoats.

或者　We are professional scapegoats.

当然,英语中有时候也会有话题突出的现象,但多半是为了达到修辞效果而进行倒装,并非常态。如：

His learning I admire, but his character I despise.

他的学识我佩服,但他的人格我鄙视。

这句英语还原成常态的主谓结构就是：I admire his learning, but I despise his character.

6. 重要信息的前置与后置

汉语句子大多遵循铺叙在前、主旨在后的行文习惯,最重要的信息通常出现在句子末尾。传说曾国藩手下将领李元度与太平军作战时屡次失利,曾国藩上奏弹劾,在奏折中说他"屡战屡败"。曾国藩的某位幕僚有意为李元度开脱,将措辞改为"屡败屡战",使得皇帝最终从轻发落。

这两种措辞初看差别不大,仔细品味就会发现,通过语序的改变,句子强调的重点也改变了。将"屡败"放在后面,强调的是失利的结果；而将"屡战"放在后面,强调的就变成了不屈不挠的顽强战斗精神了。

英语句子则恰恰相反,大多遵循的是从高潮出发的模式,最重要的信息通常出现在句子开头,然后再补充其他次要信息。例如：

Food manufacturers are flooding the UK market with new products in response to rising demand from a population hungry for "something different".

此句中最重要的信息是句首的 food manufacturers are flooding the UK market,后面的部分都是详细说明原因。译成汉语时需要调整语序,把最重要的信息放到句末。

英国人极想"尝新",要求与日俱增。针对这种情况,食品生产厂商正一个劲儿地向英国市场大量投放各种新产品。

7. 抽象与具体

英语里有大量抽象词汇,也有很多意义具体的词可以通过加前缀、后缀等手段而变成意义抽象的词。英译汉的时候如遇到这种词语,就需要通过增加具体的词汇来点明内涵。例如:

(1) The Great Wall is a must for most foreign visitors to Beijing.

长城是任何外国游客到北京的必不可少的游览项目。

(2) What they wanted most was an end of the uncertainties.

他们最需要的是结束这种动荡的局面。

以上译文中,"游览项目"和"局面"就是翻译时增加的具体词汇,它们使译文符合汉语习惯,显得通顺自然。

三、汉英文化对比

什么是文化?它的权威定义之一是由十九世纪英国人类学家爱德华·泰勒(Edward Tyler)给出的。

"Culture, ... is that complex whole which includes knowledge, belief, art, morals, law, custom, and any other capabilities and habits acquired by man as a member of society."

"文化是复杂体,包括知识、信仰、艺术、道德、法律、风俗以及其余社会上习得的能力与习惯。"

一看便知,文化实在是一个太大的范畴,要将汉英文化做系统的对比分析恐怕一部专著也不一定能圆满完成。故而这里只是大略列出几点差异,目的在于引起注意,以便平时能更主动地去了解两种文化,翻译时能更仔细地查证,从而更好地起到沟通与交流的作用。

1. 亲属称谓

汉语亲属称谓系统是世界上最复杂的称谓系统之一。中国人的亲属称谓之丰富常常让初学中文的外国朋友感到棘手。比如:

伯伯 叔叔 舅舅 姑父 姨父
姑姑 阿姨 婶婶 舅母
堂兄(弟) 堂姐(妹) 表兄(弟) 表姐(妹)

在英语中,第一排称谓只需两个词就能表达:uncle/uncle-in-law;第二排称谓同样只需两个英语词汇就能表达:aunt/aunt-in-law;第三排称谓更是浓缩到一个英语单词：cousin，既指男性又指女性。

林语堂曾这样描写慈禧太后与光绪皇帝之间的关系：

To the end, the emperor, like an eagle deprived of its wings, remained submissive to his aunt.

光绪皇帝，像个剪去翅膀的苍鹰，一直对他这位大权在握的老伯母毕恭毕敬，百依百顺。

"老伯母"一词让中文读者知道，慈禧是光绪父亲的兄长之配偶；对英文读者而言，这个亲属关系不必表述得如此细致，aunt 一词足矣。

众多严格细致的亲属称谓反映出中国人重视大家庭、特别看重亲情的文化传统。这种传统又导致了拟亲属称谓的现象产生，即用亲属称谓称呼非亲属关系的人，表示恭敬、亲热等，以拉近社交距离。比如同校同专业上下届学生之间互称师兄弟、师姐妹；地铁上不相识的成年男性为小孩让座，家长会指导小孩礼貌地表示感谢："谢谢叔叔"。翻译中意识到这种文化差异，就可以避免死译硬译带来的误解，用"He/she is in my major but a year below/behind me."以及"Thank you."分别对应以上两种情况，就可以让外国朋友理解了。

2. 成语、谚语和俗语

成语、谚语和俗语作为文化的重要载体，是人类经验与智慧的结晶，反映了不同民族的历史背景、地理环境、风俗习惯等。翻译成语、谚语和俗语时要特别注意其文化特色，才能把握得当。

中国人，尤其是汉族人，历史上以农耕为主要谋生手段，人与土地和植物的关系非常密切。而英国是一个岛国，人们的生活与大海息息相关，捕鱼业和造船业发达。所以，两国的成语和谚语即使是表达相似的道理，也会采用不同的事例。如：

（1）疾风知劲草。

A good pilot is not known when the sea is calm and the water is fair.

（2）班门弄斧

teach fish to swim

中英两国所处的地理位置不同导致了气候差异，英国下雨就比中国大部分地区频繁得多。所以当中国人说"不鸣则已，一鸣惊人"时，英国人则说"It never rains but it pours."

两国人民长期生活中形成的风俗习惯也有许多差异，比如龙作为中华民族的象征总是褒义的，中国父母望子成龙，译为"hold high hopes for one's child"。英国人喜欢狗，他们用"Love me, love my dog."来表示爱屋及乌。

此外还须考虑宗教因素。相对于中国来说，基督教的影响在英国比较深远，如：

（1）说曹操，曹操到。

Speak of angels, and you will hear their wings.

或 Talk of the devil, and he's sure to appear.（天使与魔鬼是基督教里的典型形象。）

(2) The children are in the seventh heaven with their new toys.
这些孩子因有了新的玩具而欢天喜地。（七重天乃上帝居所，言极快乐之境。）

某些成语、谚语从字面上看似乎很容易在汉英两种语言中找到对应说法，如：
out of sight, out of mind / far from eye, far from heart

乍一看，很容易让人想起中国俗语"眼不见，心不烦"，实际上这句英文的意思是长久地见不到就会慢慢忘记，即别久情疏。有一首诉说思念的英文情歌，歌名就叫 *Out of Sight, Out of Mind*。歌词前半段是这样的：

I always heard people say it,

But I guess I never fully understood it.

I thought that they meant

You'd be easy to forget.

But it's driving me crazy.

Outta sight outta mind.

You opened my eyes,

And now I can see

What you mean to me.

I was so blind.

Outta sight outta mind.

You know it hurt when you left me.

But I thought life would go on without you.

That was easier said.

Can't get you out of my head.

I don't know if I'll make it.

很明显，歌词作者挑选了人们熟悉的说法却反其道而行之，娓娓诉说相思之情不会因为恋人从视野中消失就淡化，反而由于恋人的离开更加浓烈。这样的歌名若翻译成略带贬义的"眼不见，心不烦"岂不成了笑话？如果一定要套用这个中文格式，"眼不见，心不念"可能稍好一点。所以翻译的时候切忌望文生义，而避免望文生义的办法只有多了解，多积累，多查证。

3. 中国式自谦等特有文化现象

中国文化素有自谦尊人的传统，从社交场合的简单对话就可以看出。

——"您贵姓？"

——"敝姓钱。"（或者"免贵姓钱。"）

英语文化中没有相应的习惯，所以翻译时只要译出交际意图，使之在英语中产生对等的效果即可。

——May I have your name?

——My name is …

掌握了这个原则之后,很多涉及风俗习惯的特殊情况都可以灵活处理。比如中国人送礼时说:

"一点小意思,不成敬意。"

"This is a gift for you. Hope you'll like it."

"不成敬意"这种说法若直译成英文,反而容易造成误解,不能表示敬意的礼物送出来做什么呢?直接换成英国人在类似场合常说的"Hope you'll like it"就能完成送礼示好的交际任务了。再比如席间不顾客人酒量频繁劝酒,客人告别时主人竭力挽留,这些举动当然在某种程度上体现了中国文化中的热情好客,但也会因文化差异造成对方的不解乃至不便。作为翻译,此时若能从习俗角度为双方稍作解释和协调,效果多半会比照翻原话要好。

同样,英语文化中的特有因素也会让中国人难以理解。例如:

Bright red costumes, with hats, shoes and stockings to match, are to be all the craze in the spring. Smart women will have to be careful not to yawn in the streets in case some shortsighted person is on his way to post a letter.

鲜红的时装,再配上鲜红的帽子、鞋子和袜子,是春日的时髦打扮。可是时髦的女子得小心一点,别在街头打哈欠,以防目光近视的人正在去寄信的路上。

对于中文读者来说这是件挺费解的事儿,"一身红色装扮的女子""打哈欠"与"近视眼""去寄信"不是风马牛不相及么,这二者在街上偶然碰到一起又有什么要紧呢?这种不解的根源就在于中国的邮筒是绿色的,而英国的邮筒是红色的。此时译者的加注就显得特别重要,能帮助中文读者及时感受到原文的幽默所在,并发出会心一笑。如果译者本身就不了解这种差异,仅仅从字面上翻译,原文的神采便会黯淡许多。所以,翻译的时候"以其昏昏使人昭昭"的奇迹是不存在的,只有译者自己理解到位,译文读者才可能欣赏到原文的精彩。

4. 翻译也有局限性

语言本就纷繁复杂,两种语言在转换时也可能会遗漏许多精彩之处。以中央电视台的一次采访为例:

记者:你幸福吗?

受访者:我姓曾。

中文对话虽然简单,可是里面所含的谐音、误会乃至幽默讽刺则很难用一两句简单的英文翻译出来。为了说清楚这件事,译者必须详加解释,以至最后的译文多半成为一段采访描述而非翻译。

还有更难翻译的例子:

(1) 石室诗士施氏,嗜狮,誓食十狮。施氏时时适市视狮。十时,适十狮适市。是时,适施氏适市。氏视是十狮,恃矢势,使是十狮逝也。氏拾是十狮尸,适石室。

石室湿,氏使侍拭石室。石室拭,氏始试食是十狮尸。食时,始识是狮尸,实十石狮尸,试释是事。

(2) Able was I ere I saw Elba.

例(1)中的故事情节并不复杂,妙的是故事中每个字都有相同的发音,仅在声调上有所差异。例(2)仅仅是一句话,意义上相对简单,巧的是无论从左往右还是从右往左,读起来都是一样的。翻译这两个例子时,要传达其基本意义不难,难的是原文的语言特色几乎无法保留,而语言特色在这两例中甚至比基本意义更重要。

综上所述,汉英两种语言在词法、句法上差异都甚大,它们所属的文化更是千差万别。在这两种语言之间进行翻译时,译者需要时刻对这些差异有一定的的敏感度,才可能避免死译、硬译,才可能为读者提供忠实通顺的译文,从而在中外沟通中起到桥梁作用。

翻译视听

《十分钟看懂中国》

以下哪个句子应该是视频中的英文句子?

(1) 餐桌一般是圆形的,大家能平等交谈。

a. Chinese table is usually round, everybody can talk equally with each other.

b. A Chinese dining table is usually round, allowing everyone to engage equally in conversation.

(2) 厨师注重菜肴的质、色、香、味。

a. Texture, flavor, color and aroma are key considerations for all Chinese cooks.

b. The cooks pay attention to the texture, flavor, color and aroma of the dishes.

思考与练习

1. 以下是汉语名著英译选摘,你能从中找到多少体现汉英语言差异的地方?

(1) 凤姐还欲问时,只听二门上传来云板,连叩四下,将凤姐惊醒。(《红楼梦》)
Before Xifeng could ask more, she was woken with a start by four blows in the chime bar at the second gate.

(2) 水面笼起一层薄薄透明的雾,风吹过来,带着新鲜的荷叶花香。(《荷花淀》)
Light, translucent mist had risen over the water, and the breeze was laden with the scent of fresh lotus leaves.

(3) 但今军中正缺箭用,敢烦先生监造十万支箭,以为应敌之具。(《三国演义》)

But we're rather short of arrows. Would you undertake to supply a hundred thousand for our next fight?

(4) 行者道:"嫂嫂休得推辞,我再送你个点心充饥!"又把头往上一顶。那罗刹心痛难禁,只在地上打滚,疼得她面黄唇白,只叫"孙叔叔饶命!"行者才收了手脚道:"你才认得叔叔么?我看牛大哥情上,且饶你性命!"(《西游记》)

"Don't try to say no, sister-in-law," Monkey then said, "I'm giving you a pastry in case you're hungry," He butted upwards, causing such a violent heart pain that she could only roll around on the ground, her face sallow and her lips white from agony. "Spare me, brother-in-law, spare me." Was all she could say. Only then did Monkey stop hitting and kicking. "So you call me brother-in-law, do you?" he said. "I'll spare your life for my brother's sake."

(5) 北京的冬季,地上还是积雪,灰黑色的秃树枝丫叉在晴朗的天空中,而远处有一、二风筝浮动,在我是一种惊异和悲哀。(鲁迅:《风筝》)

Often I feel deeply depressed to see the Peking winter scene when the thick snow banks up on the ground and the bare ashen tree branches thrust up against a blue sky, while in the distance one or two kites are floating casually.

(6) 老栓正在专心走路,忽地吃了一惊,远远地看着一条丁字街,明明白白地横着。他便退了几步,寻着一家关着门的铺子,蹩进门下,靠门立住了。(鲁迅:《药》)

Absorbed in his walking, Old Shuan was startled when he saw a crossroad lying distinctly ahead of him. He took a few steps backward, slipping himself in under the eaves of a closed shop, and stood against its door.

2. 比较以下英文及其译文,思考译者在词法和句法上做了哪些处理。

All languages change over a period of time, for reasons which are imperfectly understood. Or rather, since speech is really a form of human activity, like dancing or playing the piano—and not an entity in itself—it is more exact to say that each successive generation behaves linguistically in a slightly different manner from its predecessors. In his teens the young man is impatient of what he considers to be the unduly stilted vocabulary and pronunciation of his elders and he likes to show how up to date he is by the use of the latest slang, but as the years go by some of his slang becomes standard usage and in any case he slowly grows less receptive to linguistic novelties, so that by the time he reaches his forties he will probably be lamenting the slipshod speech of the younger generation, quite unaware that some of the expressions used in church and law-court were frowned upon by his own parents. In this respect, language is a little like fashions in men's dress. The informal clothes of one generation become the everyday wear of the next, and just as young doctors and bank-clerks nowadays go about their business in sports-jackets, so they allow into their normal vocabulary various expressions which were once confined to slang and familiar conversation.

  所有语言经过一段时间就要变,其变化的原因是无法完全搞清楚的。或者更确切地说,由于语言实际上是人类活动的一种形式,就像跳舞或者弹钢琴一样——其本身并非是一个实体——每一代人在语言的运用上总是与上一代人略有不同。在十几岁的年轻人看来,年龄大一点的人讲话用词过于刻板拘谨,发音很不自然。年轻人厌恶这一套,他们喜欢用最新的俚语以示自己时髦。可是,随着岁月的流逝,他们用的俚语中的一部分变成了正式用语,他们本人到头来也渐渐地不再那么容易接受语言中新奇的东西。这样,当他们年过四十,听着青年一代马虎随便的言谈也会大摇其头。殊不知,现今在教堂和法庭被人们一本正经地使用着的部分词语和发音也正是当年引得他们的父母皱眉不止的东西。在这方面,语言有点像时装。一代人有些随意的衣着会成为下一代人的日常服装。正如今天的青年医师和银行职员穿着运动衫工作一样,他们在日常用语中也吸收了各种过去一度被认为是俚语俗话的词语。

第四节 量体裁衣：语体与翻译

课前活动

下面一段文字摘自爱德华八世的禅位讲话：

...But you must believe me when I tell you that I have found it impossible to carry the heavy burden of responsibility and to discharge my duty as king as I would wish to do without the help and support of the woman I love.

请比较次日早晨，在报纸上所出现的"禅位诏书"中的这段话。二者在语体上有何不同？翻译时应分别如何处理？

...But you must accord me credence when I state to you that I found it impossible to endure the heavy burden of responsibility and to consummate the fulfillment of my stewardship as king without the assistance and cooperation of the lady upon whom I have bestowed my affection.

理论与实践

翻译不仅要在内容上忠实于原文，还要考虑原文的文体、语体和风格。本书中，文体指的是作品的体裁(genre)，如新闻报道、法律文书、散文、小说、书信和科技文章等。几种常见文体的翻译原则和方法在本书第三章中将得到详细阐述。语体(tenor of discourse)指的是语言的体式，即人们在不同场合、不同情境中所使用的话语在用词、语法等方面的特征，其主要的表现形式就是语言的正式程度(degree of formality)。风格(style)指的是作品在整体上呈现出的具有代表性的独特面貌，如语言的民族风格、时代风格、个人风格等。这三个概念既相互联系和重叠，又各有侧重。例如：法律文体的语言普遍要比书信文体正式，也就是说，前者的语体层次更高，这说明语体和文体有很强的关联性。但是，用于不同场合、起着不同功用的书信，如私人书信、求职信和业务信函等，因正式程度不同，语体层次也大不相同。一般来说，业务信函和求职信的正式程度要高于私人书信。而同样是私人书信，也因为写信者的个人表达方式与喜好的差异而呈现出不同的语言风格。

翻译时应使译文在文体、语体和风格上与原文保持一致。本节重点讨论语体与翻译的关系。

一、语体的五个层次

美国语言学家 Martin Joos 将英语语体分为五个层次，在这五个层次构成的连续体中,最正式的一端为"庄重体",而另一端为"亲密体"。"庄重体"一般见于法律文书等文体中,"亲密体"则出现在熟人之间的口语交谈中。

(1) 庄重体(frozen):法律文书或庄严的演说、宗教仪式等。
(2) 正式体(formal):推荐信、自然科学著作、教育和心理学著作等。
(3) 商洽体(consultative):新闻报道和一般文学作品等。
(4) 随意体(casual):朋友间的书信、邮件等。
(5) 亲密体(intimate):友人、熟人间的谈话等。

翻译时,要斟酌原文的语体特征,如果原文具有庄重、严肃的风格,属正式语体,译文就要给人以正式的感觉;如果原文显得通俗、随意、口语化,属非正式语体,译文就要给人以非正式的印象。

二、语体标记

如何判断文本的语体层次?除了看它的文体,还要注意各种语体标记。体现在遣词、造句、语法、称呼语等方面,随着语体层次变低,遣词由正式到随意,造句由长到短,语法由繁复到简单,称呼由繁趋简。

1. 词汇层面

1) 词源

英语词汇来源丰富,大量词汇同时有三个以上同义词或近义词,其中,最短小、最简单、口语中最常用的那个往往来自古英语,书面上常用的那个来自法语,而最正式、显得有学究气的那个则来自拉丁语或希腊语。例如下面一组词,从左到右,语体层次越来越高。

fire(古英语)	flame(法语)	conflagration(拉丁语)
rise(古英语)	mount(法语)	ascend(拉丁语)
ask(古英语)	question(法语)	interrogate(拉丁语)

2) 语域

语域(register)是指因使用场合、对象、领域等不同而出现的语言的具体变体。各种专业领域的词汇比日常词汇更正式,诗体词汇、古语词汇比普通词汇更正式。

试比较以下两组词汇,左栏与右栏词汇表达同样的意思,但是前者语体层次更高:

法律合同用语	日常词汇
prior to	before
obligation	duty
expiry	end

| 诗歌用语 | 普通词汇 |
| maiden | girl |

slumber	sleep
yonder	over there

3) 词汇形态

单个动词比短语动词更正式。如：encounter 比 come across 更正式，investigate 比 look into 更正式。

4) 词汇形式

词汇的完全形式比其缩略形式正式。如 advertisement，television，cannot 比它们的缩略形式 ad.，TV，can't 正式。

2. 句子层面

1) 单复数和代词的一致关系

正式语体要求单复数和人称代词有严格的一致关系，而较低的语体则没有这个要求。如：

(1) 正式：Everyone should do his best.

非正式：Everyone should do their best.

(2) 正式：He speaks French better than I do.

非正式：He speaks French better than me.

2) 各种连词、介词的语体层次

各种连词、介词语体层次的差异参见下面的表格。

语体层次 引导的状语类型	非　正　式	正　式
让步	anyway, though, although	in spite of, despite, notwithstanding
原因、后果	as, since, because, so	on account of, owing to, thus, therefore, hence, accordingly, consequently
条件	if, unless, suppose	supposing (that), assuming (that), providing (that), provided (that), given (that), in case (that), on condition (that)
目的	so as to	in order to, in order that

3) 前置语序与普通语序

强调前置的倒装语序比普通语序更正式。例如：

正式：Had we made adequate preparations, we might have succeeded.

非正式：If we had made adequate preparations, we might have succeeded.

4) 并列句与复合句

and，or 连接的松散的并列句更常见于非正式文体中，复合句则更多地在正式文体中出现，而分词短语或独立结构则更为正式。例如：

正式：Feeling tired, Mike went to bed early.

较正式：Mike went to bed early because he felt tired.

非正式：Mike felt tired, so he went to bed early.

5) It 起始的叙述结构与普通叙述结构

It 起始的叙述结构（如 It is noted that）的语体比普通叙述结构的语体更高。例如：

正式：It was argued that Capitalism had the seeds of destruction within itself.

非正式：They said that Capitalism had the seeds of destruction within itself.

6) 语气与语态

用虚拟语气、被动语态表示的请求比陈述语气、主动语态的请求更正式。

正式：Could I suggest that the meeting be postponed until next week?

非正式：I suggest the meeting be postponed until next week.

7) 名词化结构与动词结构

表示动作或状态的名词化结构比动词结构更正式。

正式：This leads to our pleasantly shocked realization that many of the values we unquestioningly accept are false.

非正式：We are both pleased and shocked to know many of the values we unquestioningly accept are false.

3. 称呼语差异

不同的称呼语，也因为郑重和随意之分而体现出不同的语体层次。例如：

非正式：When his father died, Peter had to get another job.

较正式：After his father's death, Peter had to change his job.

正式：On the decease of his father, Mr. Brown was obliged to seek alternative employment.

思考与练习

1. 以下为图书馆的两份告示，内容一样，但正式程度不同。请从方框中选择恰当的词汇将告示补充完整，再分别译成汉语。

A Notice by the Library

(1) It has been noted with concern that the ①_____ of books in the library has been ②_____ alarmingly. Students are requested to ③_____ themselves of the rules of the borrowing and returning of books, and to bear in

mind the needs of other students. Penalties for overdue books will in the future be strictly ④_____.

(2) The ⑤_____ of books in the library has been ⑥_____. Please make sure you know the rules for borrowing, and don't ⑦_____ that the library is for everyone's convenience. So from now on, we're going to enforce the rules strictly. You have been warned!

a. forget	b. decline	c. remind	d. enforce
e. stock	f. go down	g. number	

2. 下面是史蒂夫·乔布斯给他妻子书信的三个翻译版本,请比较并评论。

Steve Job's Love Letter

We didn't know much about each other twenty years ago. We were guided by our intuition; you swept me off my feet. It was snowing when we got married at the Ahwahnee. Years passed, kids came, good times, hard times, but never bad times. Our love and respect has endured and grown. We've been through so much together and here we are right back where we started 20 years ago—older, wiser—with wrinkles on our faces and hearts. We now know many of life's joys, sufferings, secrets and wonders and we're still here together. My feet have never returned to the ground.

【译文一】

20年前我们相知不多。我们跟着感觉走,你让我迷得飞上了天。当我们在阿瓦尼举行婚礼时天在下雪。很多年过去了,有了孩子们,有美好的时候,有艰难的时候,但从来没有过糟糕的时候。我们的爱与尊敬经历了时间的考验而且与日俱增。我们一起经历了那么多,现在我们回到20年前开始的地方——老了,也更有智慧了——我们的脸上和心上都有了皱纹。我们现在了解了很多生活的欢乐、痛苦、秘密和奇迹,我们仍然在一起。我的双脚从未落回地面。

【译文二】

二十年前,我们对彼此认识并不多。直觉引领我们彼此相遇,你让我神魂颠倒。在阿瓦尼结婚那一天,天上下着雪。多年以后,孩子一一报到,我们度过顺境、逆境,但从来没有一天不是相知相惜。我们对彼此的爱与尊重与日俱增、愈陈愈香。我们一起经历了太多事情,现在,我们又回到了二十年前的那个地方。年纪渐长、智慧渐增,脸上和心中都有了岁月的刻痕。我们经历人生的欢乐、苦痛、秘密与各种奇妙的事,而我们依然相守。我为你神魂颠倒,至今犹未回过神来。

【译文三】

20年前的我们,彼此相知甚浅;我们随心而动,随意而行。你让我目眩神迷,如入云端。当我们在阿瓦尼举行婚礼时,雪花漫天飞舞。时光荏苒,岁月如梭,孩子们的降生,那些美好的时光,那些艰难的时刻,仍历历在目,而我们却未曾经历不堪的年华。我们彼此的真爱和尊重,在岁月里沉淀发酵,与时俱浓;我们一起经历诸多风雨,阅尽世间沧桑。20年后,旧地重游,我们更苍老了,更睿智了。岁月的印记,也在我们脸上和心中留下皱褶。我们终于明白,生命中的那些快乐、痛苦、秘密和奇迹意味着什么,正因如此,我们携手共度。而身在云端的我,双脚一如既往,从未踏回世间。

第二章

翻译技巧

第一节 "辞严义正"Ⅰ：词义的选择和词类的转换

课前活动

请翻译下面的几句话。在没有上下文的情况下，你能确定它们的含义吗？

(1) —A：Should I turn left?
    —B：Right.
(2) Your cousin is on the phone.
(3) He is drawing a cart.
(4) "Oh, I don't buy it," she answers.
(5) He kissed her back.

理论与技巧

一、英汉词义的对应关系

由于自然环境、思维方式、社会历史、文化传统的不同，英汉两种语言的词汇并不是一一对应的。当然，由于客观世界的真实存在性和人们对其感知和认识上的相似性，两种语言里有大量对应词语，尤其是有关自然现象的词汇、专有名词和专业术语等，这是英汉翻译的语言基础。但是英汉两种语言中也存在大量并不对应的词语，这就给翻译增加了难度。主要有以下几种情况。

1. 假对应关系

有些英语词汇和汉语词汇在字面上显得对应，实际含义却相去甚远。产生假对应的原因，是没注意到惯用法和词的搭配。如"红茶"在英语里并不是 red tea，而是 black tea。如果照字面意思翻译，可能会闹出笑话。同样是"恶性"，"恶性循环"

是 vicious circle，而"恶性肿瘤"是 malignant tumor。

2. 一对多关系

汉语中一些表示泛称的词，英语中并没有跟它们一一对应的词，而需要用多个词来表达，如"笔"在英语中没有对应的泛称词，需要用 pen，pencil，ball pen 等具体的词来表达。

上下文和搭配两个因素也是产生一对多关系的重要原因。请看 lie 在下面不同语境中指代的不同含义。

(1) She is lying in bed with a severe cold.

她因重感冒躺在床上。

(2) The fundamental way out lies in reform and openness.

根本出路在于改革开放。

(3) The statistics must be lying.

统计数字一定有假。

(4) I like to lie on the sunny beach, basking in the sunshine.

我喜欢躺在充满阳光的海滩上晒太阳。

(5) I told my wife a white lie saying that she looked fabulous in her new clothes.

我对太太撒了个善意的谎言，称赞她穿上新衣好看极了。

3. 零对应

由于文化、环境和思维方式的区别，一种语言中的某些概念在另一种语言中可能找不到合适的对应词汇来表达。如中华民族的象征"龙"，在英语文化里是空缺的。龙常常被翻译成 dragon，但 dragon 在西方文化中被视为邪恶、凶猛的动物。（《剑桥国际英语词典》中对 dragon 的定义是：a large fierce imaginary animal, usually represented with wings, a large tail and fire coming out of its mouth。）又如"饺子"，早些时候翻译为 dumpling，但英语中 dumpling 是另一种食物，容易引起混淆。现在音译为"jiaozi"更为普遍。

在处理由于文化空缺引起零对应的情况时，常用音译的方式把这个概念表示出来，这就叫"外来词"。比如以下汉语词汇皆来自音译：

幽默 humor　　　　　浪漫 romantic
巧克力 chocolate　　　雷达 radar
马达 motor　　　　　咖啡 coffee
摩登 modern　　　　　汉堡包 hamburger
基因 gene　　　　　　麦克风 microphone

二、词义的选择和引申

1. 根据语境确定词义

同一个英语词汇用在不同的场合,中文对应的翻译常常会不同,必须充分考虑到词汇的使用场合及上下文的联系,正确选择恰当的释义。如 quarter,一般认为它的对等词是"四分之一",但请看下面的例子:

(1) She pays her rent by the quarter.
她按季度付房租。

(2) The clothes should soak for a quarter before washing.
洗这些衣服之前应浸泡一刻钟。

(3) Our basketball team began to choke up in the last quarter.
我们的篮球队在最后一节因过度紧张而开始发挥失常了。

(4) Another man put in a quarter and the computer read: "You weigh 184 pounds, you're divorced and you're on your way to Chicago."
另一个男子也投了一个25分硬币,计算机显示:"你体重184磅,你离婚了,要去芝加哥。"

从表面上来看,以上所举的 quarter 似乎"一词多义"。但仔细观察就会发现这个词仅具有一个根本意义,所谓"多义"只不过是依据上下文信息,给出符合汉语习惯的各种不同的"译法"。事实上,我们翻译时甚至不用拘泥于词典上给出的含义,而是根据语境选择词义,给出最适切的翻译。

2. 词义的引申

当无法从词典等工具书中找到直接、恰当、准确的释义时,译者可以在准确理解原文含义的基础上,结合语境,对词义进行引申。

1) 具体化引申

具体化引申是指将原文中较抽象、概括、笼统的词汇和结构引申为较为具体的词汇和结构,以避免译文含混不清或不符合译入语的表达习惯。

(1) Dawn breaking over the islands, very beautiful in a soft grey light with many clouds. There is a transparency about the light here which cannot be described or painted.
曙色中的海岛美极了,晨曦柔和,彩云片片。那澄澈的光影是无法描绘的。

英文中抽象名词 transparency 被译为"澄澈的光影",化虚为实,再现了原文清新、柔和的美景。

(2) When the Sheridans were little they were forbidden to set foot there because of the revolting language and of what they might catch.
谢里登家里的人,小时候是不准去那儿的,生怕学到一些下流话,或沾染上什么毛病。

(3) He is the admiration of the whole school.

他是全校所敬佩的人。

2) 抽象化引申

原文中一些比较具体的词,在译文中如果找不到对等的表达,可根据需要,进行抽象化或概括化处理。

(1) The interest rates have seesawed between 10 and 15 percent.

利率在10%和15%之间不断波动。

句中 seesaw 的意思是跷跷板一上一下的交替摆动,译成汉语时可抽象化为"波动"。

值得一提的是,汉语形象性词语(如比喻、成语、谚语、歇后语)相当丰富。汉语常常借助这类生动、具体的词语来表达英语抽象、笼统的意义。如果英文中无法找到对应的形象化表达,可进行抽象化处理。例如:

(2) 他这一阵心头如同十五个吊桶打水,七上八下,老是宁静不下来。(周而复:《上海的早晨》)

His mind was in a turmoil these days and he was quite unable to think straight.

3) 修辞性引申

在文学翻译中,有时为了使译文增色,除了真实地再现原文包括的内容外,还可运用汉语中形象、生动的成语等进行适当的修辞性引申。

(1) You know what the worst part is? You're sitting here, perfectly happy, and he's at home, a blubbering messiness.

你知道最让人受不了的是什么吗?你坐在这里,眉开眼笑;而他却窝在家,以泪洗面。

为使译文简洁通畅,科技翻译中也可用修辞性引申。例如:

(2) Computers come in a wide variety of sizes and capabilities.

计算机大小不一,性能各异。

4) 语用引申

翻译时,不仅要看到词汇的指称意义,还要注意其语用意义,将原文中的弦外之音(implication)翻译出来。例如:

"You chicken!" he cried, looking at Tom with contempt.

"你这个胆小鬼!"他轻蔑地看着汤姆大叫道。

这里 chicken 的含义是"懦夫、胆小鬼",而不是其指称意义"小鸡",翻译时要进行语用引申,准确转达原文含义。

3. 词义的缩小和扩大

由于英汉两种语言表达习惯不同,在进行翻译时,有时需要扩大或缩小原文词汇的表面词义,准确地表达其内涵。例如:

(1) A bridge must be built which is capable of being opened in order to allow the river or canal traffic to pass.

桥梁必须建成开启式的,以便江河或江河的船只通过。

英文句子里 traffic 原意是"交通、运输、运输量",但在这里,通过缩小其外延,译为"船只",译文更加清晰、准确。

有时,又需要将原文涵义扩大。例如:

(2) Because of the circuitous and directional flow of waterways, railways often have an energy advantage over barges.

由于河道迂回曲折并具有方向性,铁路运输对于水运而言,常具有节能的优势。

这个句子里的 railway(铁路)和 barge(驳船),译为外延更宽泛的"铁路运输"和"水运",更好地体现了作者的原意,也更符合汉语的表达习惯。

4. 注意词汇的褒贬和感情色彩

翻译时还要注意英汉两种语言中词汇包含的感情色彩,根据上下文判断翻译时该用褒义词还是该用贬义词。如《毛泽东选集》第五卷中的一个例子:

他们讲唯心论,我们讲唯物论。

They preach idealism, while we advocate materialism.

这里"讲"字分别译为 preach(贬义)和 advocate(褒义)。

三、词类的转换

英汉词类在使用频率上有所不同。相比较而言,汉语使用动词的频率更高,英语使用名词和介词的频率更高。主要原因是英语以一个主要动词为句子的中轴,而用汉语表达同样的内容则需要一组短句,包含更多动词。同时英语中大量使用介词,而汉语中则较少使用介词。

英汉互译时应根据两种语言的特点和具体情况的需要,灵活使用词类转换技巧,使译文更加通顺、地道。常见的词类转换技巧如下。

1. 英语名词结构与汉语动词结构的转换

(1) Too much exposure to TV programs will do great harm to the eyesight of children.

孩子们看电视过多会大大地损坏视力。

(2) 农民缺乏培训,许多农场生产效率低,使得绝大多数农村人口在国内处于不利的地位。

Inadequate training for farmers and the low productivity of many farms place the vast majority of country dwellers in a disadvantageous position in their own country.

有时,英语中的动词也可根据需要译为汉语中的名词。例如:

(3) Formality has always <u>characterized</u> their relationship.

他们之间的关系,有一个<u>特点</u>,就是以礼相待。

2. 英语介词和汉语动词的相互转换

(1) There are stories too <u>of</u> early African voyages to America.

另外,还有一些传说,<u>谈到</u>非洲人最初航海到美洲来的情形。

(2) I was <u>on</u> my way home from tramping <u>about</u> the streets, my drawings <u>under</u> my arm, when I found myself <u>in front of</u> the Mathews Gallery.

我挟着画稿在街上兜了一圈,回家的路上无意中发现自己逛到了马太画廊的门口。

3. 其他词类转换

(1) Originally Ingrid Bergman was from Sweden.

英格丽·褒曼的原籍是瑞典。(副词→名词)

(2) She recognized the <u>absurdity</u> of dealing with them through intermediaries.

她认识到,通过中间人和他们打交道是愚蠢可笑的。(名词→形容词)

(3) Blood work finally came back. I'm perfectly normal—a little <u>heavy</u> on the iron.

血液检查的结果出来了,我完全正常,只是铁含量有点超标。(形容词→动词)

课堂练习

1. 以下英汉词汇的翻译有什么问题?正确的说法是什么?

　(1) normal university　普通大学

　(2) love handles　爱的把手

　(3) break a leg　断了一条腿

　(4) eat one's words　食言

2. 以下"送"字用英语怎么表达?

　(1) 送某人一本书

　(2) 送牛奶

　(3) 送行

　(4) 将卫星送上天

　(5) 送罪犯上法庭审判

3. 以下翻译正确吗?如果有误,请纠正。

　(1) 开飞机　drive a plane

　(2) 增加体重　add to weight

　(3) 增加预算　add budget

　(4) 抓紧时间　grasp time firmly

(5) 介绍经验　introduce one's experience
(6) 传授知识　teach knowledge
(7) 吃食堂　eat the canteen
(8) 听电话　listen the telephone
(9) 三角债　triangle debts
(10) 来信写道　the letter writes
(11) 学习知识　learn knowledge
(12) 扣帽子　put a cap on

4. 以下"香"字用英语怎么表达？
(1) 香气扑鼻
(2) 香喷喷的饭菜
(3) 睡得很香
(4) 香闺
(5) 香车美女
(6) 香消玉殒
(7) 香艳
(8) 香火传承

翻译视听

看视频，将你听到的英语原文写出来，注意比较原文翻译成汉语后，在词类上的变化。

(1) 因为 Gaga 才是来唱歌的。

(2) 然后他说："你至少会唱一首吧。"

(3) 我来这里只是为了搞笑。

(4) 我不会让节奏稍稍慢下来，以配合我下台走向一位美女。

(5) 我不会对她唱歌，不会把她当作今晚唯一的观众。

第二节 "辞严义正"Ⅱ：词的增减

课前活动

有人说不管是英译汉还是汉译英，译文总会比原文长一点。你赞成吗？为什么？

理论与实践

由于英汉两种语言表达方式的差异，翻译时不仅需要转换词类，有时还要在词量上进行增减。词汇增减的原则是"增（减）词不增（减）义"。

虽然英汉互译时，涉及句法结构的增、减词现象十分普遍，如补充省略的主语等，这在后面句法翻译的章节中会得到详尽阐述。本节主要从语义层面讨论增、减词法。主要有以下几种情况。

一、增词法

1. 增补潜在词

英语中存在大量不及物动词，其中一些译成汉语时显得语义不明，这时要将其隐含的宾语翻译出来。例如：

(1) And maybe you should listen and drink in moderation or not at all.

也许你应该听从建议，适量饮酒或者一点都不喝。

(2) He picks up 5-year-old Jilly after school, and in the evening gives her a bath and reads to her.

放学后他接5岁的吉莉回家，晚上给她洗澡并给她念书。

作为一种意会的语言，汉语句子中常有些暗含而无须明言的词语，要将其隐含的意思翻译出来。例如：

(3) 感冒可以通过人的手传染。

Flu can be spread through hand contact.

译文补上 contact，因为原文的含义实际上是"通过手的接触"。

2. 增补省略的词

在英语和汉语中都存在省略的情况。英语中常见的是将对等结构中相同的部分省略。比如：

(1) Prosperity discovers vices and adversity virtues.

兴旺时现邪恶,艰难时显美德。

原文中将 and 连接的对等结构中后面部分的谓语省略,以避免重复。汉语则将其补全,语义完整,并形成结构和音韵上的对称美。

汉语重表意,省略的情况也比较常见,其中典型的例子是四字成语,通过汉字的简单排列构成,依赖读者意会来理解。遇到这类情况,翻译时需要增加词语,以表达内在意义,明确概念关系,有时还需要提供背景知识。例如:

(2) 班门弄斧

show off one's proficiency with axe before Luban

3. 增补语法词

根据两种语言在语法上的不同要求进行增词。英语通过名词的单、复数变化表示数量,而汉语则通过数量词来表示数量,因此英语翻译成汉语时,要补足数量词。例如:

(1) A stream was winding its way through the valley into the river.

一弯溪水蜿蜒流过山谷,汇到江里去了。

英语动词有各种时态变化,汉语动词则没有。翻译时要增词以揭示时态的含义。例如:

(2) We can learn what we didn't know.

我们能学会我们原来不懂的东西。

4. 增补修饰性和解释性词语

The farmer snapped a stick and put it into the fire.

农民"啪"的一声折断了一根树枝,把它放进火里。

5. 增补范畴词

汉语倾向以具体的形象表达抽象的内容。英译汉时可以使英语抽象的概念具体化,根据具体的语境加上"方法""现象""局势""状态""情况""政策""做法""习俗""精神""态度"和"问题"等范畴词,使译文含义清晰,行文流畅。反之,汉译英时把整个名词词组译成英语中的抽象名词即可。

(1) This test was set up to demonstrate the stability and precision of Volvo dynamic steering.

本测试是用来证明沃尔沃汽车动态转向系统的稳定性和精确度。

(2) 我们必须共同珍惜和维护亚洲地区来之不易的和平稳定局面。

We must cherish and safeguard the hard-won peace and stability in Asia.

6. 增补某些概括性的词语

(1) The paper discussed language teaching and language research.

论文讨论了语言教学和语言研究(两方面)的内容。

(2) Note that the words "foxy" "mean" and "generous" require explanation.

请注意:"狡猾的""吝啬的"和"慷慨的"(这三个词)需要解释一下。

7. 增补连接词

汉语是"意合"的语言,上下文之间的逻辑联系往往不言而明。而英语重"形合",大量使用连接词。汉语译为英语时,需要适当增加连接词。例如:

(1) 跑得了和尚跑不了庙。

The monk can run away, <u>but</u> the temple can not.

英译汉时,为了保证译文的逻辑性,有时也需要适当增加连接词。

(2) Heat from the sun stirs up the atmosphere, generating winds.

太阳发出的热量搅动大气,<u>于是</u>产生了风。

二、减词法

1. 减去对偶同义词中的某一个词

汉语中使用对偶同义词的情况比较普遍,即两个词汇并列出现,指代相同或相似的意思,形成匀称对仗的结构,以加强语气。翻译时不必字字对应,可以省略重复的词汇,只要译出中心意思即可。例如:

(1) 农历5月5日的端午节是为了纪念古代诗人和忠臣屈原,他被昏庸君主<u>贬官放逐</u>而抱石投江自尽。

The Dragon Boat Festival on the 5th day of the 5th lunar month is celebrated in memory of Quyuan, an ancient poet and loyal minister who drowned himself while <u>in exile</u> from a corrupt court.

中国古代的"贬官"其实就是"放逐"到偏远地区的意思,这里属同义复指,可简化译成:be sent into exile / be in exile。

相似的例子还有:

捕风捉影	catch at shadows	花言巧语	fine words
街谈巷议	gossip	冷言冷语	sarcastic remarks
水深火热	in deep waters	贪官污吏	corrupt officials
土崩瓦解	fall apart	医德医风	medical ethics
字斟句酌	weigh every word	自吹自擂	blow one's own trumpet
自言自语	talk to oneself		

英语某些语体中也有运用"对偶同义词"的现象,翻译时也可以省掉同义词中的一个。例如:

(2) The treaty was pronounced <u>null and void</u>.

条约被宣布无效。

2. 减去冗余的词

英语忌讳相同信息的重复,翻译时应避免冗余语病(redundancy)。例如:

吸收外来移民,是加拿大长期奉行的国策。

译文一：Admitting immigrants from other countries has become a national policy long practised by Canada.

译文二：Admitting immigrants has become a national policy long practised by Canada.

原文中 immigrants 所指的"移民"本身就包含着"来自其他国家"的含义。因此应当把 from other countries 这个短语删去。

3. 减去连词和介词

作为一种"形合"的语言，英语中大量使用连词和介词，译为汉语时，可根据需要省译。

(1) They waited a long time before he suddenly stepped out on the balcony and raised a hand in salute.

人们等了很久，忽然他走了出来，站在阳台上，举起手敬礼。

(2) Jerram was secretary to Combined Operations Headquarters in 1943, and from 1943 to 1945 he was Comptroller. He retired in 1945, and from 1958 was a Deputy Lieutenant for Cornwall.

1943 年，杰拉姆任联合作战指挥部秘书。1943 年至 1945 年，他任监察官。1945 年退伍。1958 年起，任康瓦尔郡副郡长。

4. 减去代词

英语倾向于多用代词，凭借指代关系传递逻辑信息。汉语则倾向于凭借复述传递逻辑信息。因此，应注意在汉语译文中适当减去代词。

(1) Driving on the left is strange at first but you get used to it.

一开始，在马路左边开车可能很奇怪，可是习惯了就好了。

(2) Fight when you can win; move away when you cannot win.

打得赢就打，打不赢就走。

(3) But it's the way I am, and try as I might, I haven't been able to change it.

但我就是这个脾气，虽然几经努力，却未能改变过来。

5. 减去冠词

(1) A candle lights others and consumes itself.

蜡烛照亮了别人，却燃尽了自己。

(2) A bird in the hand is worth two in the bush.

一鸟在手胜过双鸟在林。

注意在某些场合，冠词不能省略。例如：

(1) He left without saying a word.

他一句话不说就走了。

(2) He said he was getting a dollar a mile.

他说他每开一英里就赚一美元。

佳译描红

要做好翻译,必须亲自动手进行大量的实践,取得第一手的经验。但是只靠自己的实践是不够的,还必须借助于别人的经验。请先通读下文,再翻译。注意画线的句子的翻译。然后对照参考译文再读一遍,注意译文对词汇的处理技巧。

Is More Growth Really Better?

A number of writers have raised questions about the desirability of faster economic growth as an end in itself. ① Yet faster growth does mean more wealth, and to most people the desirability of wealth is beyond question. "I've been rich and I've been poor—and I can tell you, rich is better," a noted stage personality is said to have told an interviewer, and most people seem to have the same attitude about the economy as a whole. ② To those who hold this belief, a healthy economy is one that is capable of turning out vast quantities of shoes, food, cars, and TV sets. An economy whose capacity to provide all these things is not expanding is said to have succumbed to the disease of stagnation. ③

Yet the desirability of further economic growth for a society that is already wealthy has been questioned on grounds that undoubtedly have a good deal of validity. ④ It is pointed out that the sheer increase in quantity of products has imposed an enormous cost on society in the form of pollution, crowding, proliferation of wastes that need disposal, and debilitating psychological and social effects. ⑤ It is said that industry has transformed the satisfying and creative tasks of the artisan into the mechanical and dehumanizing routine of the assembly line. It has dotted our roadsides with junkyards, filled our air with smoke, and poisoned our food with dangerous chemicals. The question is whether the outpouring of frozen foods, talking dolls, radios, and headache remedies is worth its high cost to society.

As one well-known economist put it: the continued pursuit of economic growth by Western Societies is more likely on balance to reduce rather than increase social welfare. Technological innovations may offer to add to men's material opportunities. But by increasing the risks of their obsolescence it adds also to their anxiety. Swifter means of communications have the paradoxical effect of isolating people; increased mobility has led to more hours commuting; increased automobilization to increased separation; more television to less communication. ⑥ In consequence, people know less of their neighbors than ever before. ⑦

Virtually every economist agrees that these concerns are valid, though many question whether economic growth is their major cause. Nevertheless, they all emphasize that pollution of air and water, noise and congestion, and the mechanization of the work process are very real and very serious problems. There is every reason for society to undertake programs that grapple with these problems. ⑧

  end 目的
  personality 名人
  succumb 屈服
  validity 有效性，根据
  debilitate 使衰弱
  dehumanize 使失去人性
  obsolescence 过时
  congestion 拥堵

  beyond question 毋庸置疑的
  capacity 能力
  stagnation 停滞
  proliferation 激增
  artisan 工匠
  on balance 总体来说
  paradoxical 矛盾的
  grapple with 与……格斗，努力克服

【注释】

① end 在此句中是"目的"的意思。as an end in itself 表示"以经济发展本身为目的"。

② personality 意思是"名人"，而不是"人格"。

③ 此句中定语从句怎样翻译更贴切？请参考本章第五节"定语从句的翻译"。

④ 对这样一个长句的翻译，应力图在理解的基础上简洁地表达句子的意思，并符合汉语的表达习惯。长句的翻译方法在后面会学习。

⑤ pollution 和 crowding 如果简单地译为"污染"和"拥挤"，听起来不大顺耳，注意参考译文中的处理方法。

⑥ paradoxical 的意思是"自相矛盾的"，修饰名词 effect，表示实际效果与预期相反。

⑦ 此句直译为"人们比任何时候都更不了解他们的邻居"，很拗口，译文中是如何处理的呢？这种正话反说的翻译技巧在本章第三节里有介绍。

⑧ There is every reason to... 意为"有一切理由（做某事）"，中文一般不会这样表达，你可以换个说法吗？

【参考译文】

经济发展越快越好吗？

近年来，不少人或撰文或著书，已经提出质疑：为经济增长而发展经济，究竟有无必要？诚然，经济增长得越快的确意味着更多的财富，而且大多数人都追求财富，这是毋庸置疑的。"富裕也罢，贫穷也罢，我都经历过。说实话，富裕当然胜过贫穷。"一位知名演员曾这样向采访者坦言。大多数人在整体上对经济似乎也持同

样观点。他们认为,健康的经济必然能够生产出大批量的鞋子、食品、汽车和电视机。当某个经济体的这种产出能力不再扩大,人们就认为它遭遇了经济停滞。

然而对于一个已经非常富足的社会而言是否有必要再一味追求发展,人们对此的质疑,无疑是有充分理由的。一味地追求产品数量的增长已经让社会付出了巨大的代价。比如环境污染,交通拥挤,需特殊处理废物的激增,以及由此造成的负面心理及社会影响。人们认为,工业化的出现,已经把以往工匠们给人以享受的创造性工作,变成了流水线上毫无人性的机械化操作。它使街头堆满了垃圾,空气中弥漫着烟雾,食品中残留着有毒农药。问题在于,那些大量的冷冻食品、说话娃娃、收音机和止痛药能否弥补工业化给社会造成的巨大代价。

正如一位著名的经济学家所言:西方社会一味地追求经济发展,总体看来,非但没有优化人们的社会生活,相反有恶化趋势。科技创新也许给人们带来了物质上的满足,但是由于更新换代的速度太快,反而使人们倍感焦虑;通讯方式更加快捷了,人们却更加孤独了;社会流动性增强了,人们反而疲于奔命;汽车更加普及了,人们反而更加疏远了;看电视的时间多了,人们交流的机会少了。结果人们与周围邻居之间从来没有像现在这样陌生。

几乎所有的经济学家都认为这种关注并非杞人忧天,尽管很多人并不认为经济的增长就是罪魁祸首。然而他们一致强调:水和空气污染、噪音、交通拥挤、机械化的工作等问题的确是很严重的现实问题。社会确实没有任何理由不尽一切努力解决好这些问题。

第三节　挪转乾坤：翻译中的视角转换

课前练习

以下汉语常用语在英语里经常怎么说？
(1) 别难过了。
(2) 别惹我。
(3) 别生气。
(4) 在我家甭客气。
(5) 少管闲事。
(6) 请勿践踏草地。

理论与技巧

一、正反角度转换

汉英思维的差异，不仅体现在词法和句法上，也表现在表达观点的不同角度上。

比如，在表示劝导和建议时，汉语中常用否定句。如"别难过了。""在我家甭客气。"这是因为在中国文化习俗中崇尚集体主义，无论是长辈对晚辈，还是朋友对朋友，直接的行为劝止都被视为好意。译为英语时，如果直接转换成以否定词开头表示阻止的句子，如"Don't be sad."和"Don't be polite at my home."则有冒犯之嫌。这是由于英语文化中崇尚个体主义，注意人与人的心理距离。以上在汉语中用否定句表达的劝导和建议，在英文中往往用更含蓄的方式正面表达为"Please cheer up."和"Make yourself at home."

由于种种已知和不甚明了的原因，汉语和英语在描述同一件事物时，角度往往略有差异，甚至完全相反。这给我们的翻译造成了困难。意识到这种差异的存在，我们在进行翻译时，如果正面译不顺，不妨试着从反面着笔，或能峰回路转，豁然开朗。请看下面的例子：

(1) If it rains in Cleveland today, volunteers will stand in lines with umbrellas to <u>keep voters dry</u>.

直接按原文的表达方式来翻译，译文是这样的：
如果今天克里弗兰下雨，志愿者将排队撑着伞，以保持选民干燥。

这样的句子是很令人费解的。但如果换成否定句式,就很通顺了。

如果今天克里弗兰下雨,志愿者将排队撑着伞,以免选民淋湿。

更多例子:

(2) Suddenly he heard a sound behind him, and realized he was <u>not alone</u> in the garage.

他突然听见后面有声响,意识到车库里还有别人。

(3) Law is <u>no respecter of</u> persons.

法律面前,人人平等。

(4) 他的照片拍得不错。

He has taken an <u>excellent photo</u>.

另外,还要注意,英语里还有大量的短语或搭配,表面上没有否定词,却暗含否定意义,如 far from, ignorant of, beyond 等,也需要译者进行正反转换,译文才能通顺。

(5) The newspaper accounts are <u>far from</u> being true.

报纸的报道远非事实。

(6) 那里的县委不了解实情。

The County Party Committee there <u>is ignorant of</u> what happened.

(7) 事实真相同你想的完全不同。

The truth is <u>quite other than</u> what you think.

(8) It was <u>beyond his power</u> to sign such a contract.

他无权签订这种合同。

下面汉语句子的翻译中,以正说词替代反说词,更符合英语的语感及语言表达习惯。

(9) 黛玉<u>不知以何称呼</u>。(《红楼梦》第三回,杨宪益、戴乃迭译)

Daiyu was <u>at a loss</u> how to address her.

(10) <u>毋庸置疑</u>,上个世纪世界航天和航空工业取得了辉煌的成就。

<u>It is beyond doubt</u> that brilliant achievements were made in aviation and space industry in the world during the last century.

二、相对性转换

视角转换不仅限于正反之间的转换,还包括转换观察的角度和表达的切入点。英汉两种文化里观察和叙述事物的角度不尽相同,当同一角度叙事显得生硬不自然时,不妨跳出窠臼,换一个与之相对的角度来表达原文。例如:

(1) She has been a widow only six months, and it is too soon for her to remarry.

译文一:她成为寡妇才不过半年,就要改嫁,未免太快了。

译文二:她丈夫去世才不过半年,就要改嫁,未免太快了。

译文一跟原文一样,从"她"的角度来叙述,但"成为寡妇"显得不太自然。译文二利用事物的相对性,从"丈夫去世"的角度来叙述,读来就顺畅多了。

(2) "You ever eat one of those things?" asked Dillon, nodding toward the ducks.

译文一:"你吃过这玩意儿吗?"狄龙对鸭子点点头,问道。

文中狄龙"nodding toward the ducks"是为了让对方知道,"这玩意儿"指的是湖面上的鸭子。但译为"对鸭子点头",显得不太清楚,且容易造成歧义,似乎是在跟鸭子打招呼。其实,点头时下巴也会动,只要转换观察角度,将"点头"译为"抬下巴",或者反过来,表达为"扬头",就很容易理解了。

译文二:"你吃过这玩意儿吗?"狄龙朝湖面扬了扬头/抬了抬下巴/一摆头,问道。

三、主动与被动转换

请比较以下几组汉英句子:

(1) 狡兔死,走狗烹。

When the cunning hare is killed, the hound is boiled.

(2) 他分到了一套房子。

He was allotted an apartment.

(3) It is generally accepted that the experiences of the child in his first years largely determine his character and later personality.

人们普遍认为,孩子们的早年经历在很大程度上决定了他们的性格以及未来的人品。

英语中被动句式出现频率远高于汉语。这是因为英语强调主、谓语在逻辑上的一致性,为了配合主语,经常需要使用被动语态;另外,英语中较多使用客观事物做主语,不必说出主动者,这也是被动语态出现频繁的原因。但英语中使用被动语态的场合,汉语中往往以主动形式出现。因此,将英语译为汉语时,根据需要,常常要变换语态。具体转换技巧如下。

1. 译成汉语主动句

1) 形式上是主动句,表达被动意义

Another middle school has been set up in our district.

我们区又办了一所中学。

2) 译成带表语的主动句——"是……的"

Rainbows are formed when sunlight passes through small drops of water in the sky.

彩虹是阳光穿过空气中的小水滴时形成的。

3) 含主语从句的被动句译为主动句

What we say here will not be long remembered.

我们在这里所讲的话,人们不会长久记住。

以 it 作为形式主语的英语句子,翻译时常要转为主动形式,有时可加上"有人""大家""我们"等不确定主语。例如:

(1) It is suggested that meeting be put off till next Monday。

有人建议会议推迟到下星期一举行。

(2) It is well known that natural light is actually made up of many colors.

众所周知,自然光其实是由许多种颜色构成的。

这类句型还有:

It is said that... 据说(有人说,人们说)……

It should be pointed out that... 必须指出的是……

It must be admitted that... 必须承认……

2. 译成汉语被动句

汉语中也有一些被动句,但不像英语那样有统一、固定的形式,除"被"这样的字眼外,还可以用"受、挨、遭、由、叫、给、为"等字词表示被动。

1) 译成"被""遭受"等词

North China was hit by an unexpected heavy rain, which caused severe flooding.

华北地区遭受了一场意外的大雨袭击,引起了严重的水灾。

2) 译成"把""使"和"由"字句

(1) The famous hotel had been practically destroyed by the fire.

大火使这家著名的旅馆几乎全部毁坏。

(2) The plan is going to be examined first by the research group.

计划将先由研究小组加以研究。

3. 译成无主语句

汉语中,往往用施事者做主语,由于施事者是人这一点是不言而喻的,所以常常省略,不说出来反而更自然,因此常常可以用无主句翻译英语被动句。例如:

Some measures must be taken to control the water pollution.

必须采取某些措施来控制水污染。

在汉译英时,则要注意体会句子的被动含义,根据需要进行主动与被动转换,使译文地道、准确。例如:

(1) 一开机,就发现有病毒。

Viruses were found as soon as the computer was powered on.

(2) 他昨天上学路上淋雨了。

Yesterday he was caught in the rain on his way to school.

课堂练习

请将下列对应的英汉谚语连线，注意正反表达角度的差异：

(1) 天无绝人之路。　　　　　　a. You can't make omelet without breaking eggs.

(2) 人不可貌相。　　　　　　　b. Many kiss the baby for the nurse's sake.

(3) 有失才有得。　　　　　　　c. Don't poke your nose into others' business.

(4) 同行是冤家。　　　　　　　d. Every cloud has a silver lining.

(5) 一分耕耘，一分收获。　　　e. A good conscience is a soft pillow.

(6) 少管闲事。　　　　　　　　f. Beauty is but skin deep.

(7) 醉翁之意不在酒。　　　　　g. No pains, no gains.

(8) 为人不做亏心事，夜半敲门心不惊。　h. Two of a trade did never agree.

佳译描红

请通读下面的一段文字，先口头翻译一下，然后再比照参考译文谈谈你的看法。特别注意画线部分句子的翻译。

I Have a Dream（excerpt）

by Martin Luther King, Jr.

And so even though we face the difficulties of today and tomorrow, I still have a dream. It is a dream deeply rooted in the American dream.

I have a dream that one day this nation will rise up and live out the true meaning of its creed: "We hold these truths to be self-evident, that all men are created equal."

I have a dream that one day on the red hills of Georgia, the sons of former slaves and the sons of former slave owners will be able to sit down together at the table of brotherhood.

I have a dream that one day even the state of Mississippi, a state sweltering with the heat of injustice, sweltering with the heat of oppression, will be transformed into an oasis of freedom and justice.

I have a dream that my four little children will one day live in a nation where they will not be judged by the color of their skin but by the content of their character.

I have a dream today!

I have a dream that one day, down in Alabama, with its vicious racists, with its governor having his lips dripping with the words of "interposition" and "nullification"—one day right there in Alabama little black boys and black girls will be able to join hands with little white boys and white girls as sisters and brothers.

I have a dream today!

I have a dream that one day every valley shall be exalted, and every hill and mountain shall be made low, the rough places will be made plain, and the crooked places will be made straight, "and the glory of the Lord shall be revealed and all flesh shall see it together".

This is our hope, and this is the faith that I go back to the South with.

With this faith, we will be able to hew out of the mountain of despair a stone of hope. With this faith, we will be able to transform the jangling discords of our nation into a beautiful symphony of brotherhood. With this faith, we will be able to work together, to pray together, to struggle together, to go to jail together, to stand up for freedom together, knowing that we will be free one day.

【参考译文】

我有一个梦想(节选)

马丁·路德·金

尽管眼下困难重重,但我依然怀有一个梦。这个梦深深植根于美国梦之中。我梦想有一天,这个国家将会奋起,实现其立国信条的真谛:"我们认为这些真理不言而喻:人人生而平等。"

我梦想有一天,在佐治亚州的红色山冈上,昔日奴隶的儿子能够同昔日奴隶主的儿子同席而坐,亲如手足。

我梦想有一天,甚至连密西西比州——一个非正义和压迫的热浪逼人的荒漠之州,也会改造成为自由和公正的青青绿洲。

我梦想有一天,我的四个孩子将生活在一个不是以皮肤的颜色,而是以品格的优劣作为评判标准的国家里。

我今天怀有一个梦。

我梦想有一天,亚拉巴马州会有所改变,尽管那儿种族主义者猖獗,尽管该州州长现在仍滔滔不绝地说什么要对联邦法令提出异议和拒绝执行,但总有一天,那儿的黑人儿童能够和白人儿童兄弟姐妹般地携手并行。

我今天怀有一个梦。

我梦想有一天,深谷弥合,高山夷平,歧路化坦途,曲径成通衢,"上帝的光华再现,普天下生灵共谒"。

　　这是我们的希望。这是我将带回南方去的信念。有了这个信念,我们就能从绝望之山开采出希望之石。有了这个信念,我们就能把这个国家的嘈杂刺耳的争吵声,变为充满手足之情的悦耳交响曲。有了这个信念,我们就能一同工作,一同祈祷,一同斗争,一同入狱,一同维护自由,因为我们知道,我们终有一天会获得自由。

第四节 化整为零：英语长句的翻译

课前活动

请你猜一下，世界上最长的英语句子包含多少个单词？

理论与技巧

在表达比较复杂的概念时，英语习惯用复合长句，其中从句、非谓语动词和介词短语围绕主句层层附着，形成错综复杂，同时重点突出、层次分明的"树状"结构；而汉语则不然，汉语中常常使用若干短句，短句之间语法关系较松散，彼此制约性较弱，没有明显的主从关系，犹如竹枝节节升高，故有人称为"竹状"结构。因此，在进行英译汉时，要依据两种语言之间的差异，将英语的长句分解，化整为零，翻译成汉语的短句。

在拆分过程中，由于具体情况不同，拆分的方式也各异。根据是否需要调整语序，是否需要打破原有的句子结构，分为以下几种情况：顺拆、逆拆、抽词拆译，以及重构拆译。下面分别介绍这几种长句翻译技巧。

一、保留语序——顺拆法

当英语句子的逻辑顺序跟汉语一致时，翻译时可以顺势拆句，也就是按英语句子的语序把英语长句化整为零，按意群将长句断开译成若干汉语分句。例如：

There is nothing more disappointing to a hostess who has gone to a lot of trouble or expense than to have her guest so interested in talking politics or business with her husband that he fails to notice the flavor of the coffee, the lightness of the cake, or the attractiveness of the house, which may be her chief interest and pride.

最令女主人失望的是，她花了许多心思和费用来招待客人，可是这位客人只顾津津有味地与她的丈夫谈政治、谈生意，却没注意到香喷喷的咖啡，松软的糕点，或房间内讲究的陈设，而这些可能才是她最感兴趣和引为自豪的。

在遇到长句时，应首先考虑能否把此句化整为零，在采用切断法时，为保证逻辑通畅，可适当运用汉语的关联词。

二、颠倒语序——逆拆法

由于英汉两种思维方式的差异，有时英语的语序跟汉语并不一致。当涉及逻辑关系时,英语常常直截了当,先果后因,而汉语则从因到果顺理推移,从解释到结论,从条件到结果。在叙和议的关系上,英语一般先表态后叙事,而汉语一般先交代事情,后发表议论。在描绘场景时,英语先焦点后远景,由里及外;汉语则由远及近,由次及主。叙事时,汉语常常依照时间顺序,英语则比较不受时间顺序的限制。

基于以上差异,在翻译英语长句时,如果跟汉语习惯的语序不一致,就需要在将其拆分成若干短句后,按汉语习惯表达法进行重新安排,结果译句中各分句的顺序与原句中的相反。例如:

(1) Such is human nature that a great many people are often willing to sacrifice higher pay for the privilege of becoming white collar workers. (议论→叙述)

许多人宁愿牺牲比较高的工资以换取成为白领工作者的社会地位,此乃人之常情。(叙述→议论)

(2) There are songs that come free from the blue-eyed grass, from the dust of a thousand country roads. (事件→背景)

从开满蝴蝶花的草丛中,从千百条乡间道路的尘埃中,常有关不住的歌声飞出来。(背景→事件)

三、译词成句——抽词拆译法

英语句子中的一些词和结构,如名词、过去分词等,信息承载量较大,对于这种信息"超载"的结构,翻译时可以将其从句中拆出来另行处理。例如:

(1) Flying from Australia to Hongkong, the tourist group then traveled thousands of interest-filled miles through China by train.

旅行团从澳大利亚乘飞机到香港,然后乘火车在中国旅行了数千里,<u>一路上兴趣盎然</u>。

(2) "We won an open and honest fight," he told the <u>victory rally</u> as tears rolled down his cheeks.

<u>支持者</u>(在莫斯科克里姆林宫旁的马涅日广场)集会庆祝获胜。普京在讲话时眼含热泪,表示这一战赢得公平诚实。(括号里为译者增补的背景信息。)

四、句子重组——重构拆译法

英语中有些句子,含有被动语态、插入成分、倒装,结构较复杂,无法顺拆;从句层层环扣,不易切断其间的连接关系,逆拆也不解决问题;含大量静态词汇和介词结构,在汉语里找不到相似的表达方式。拆译也往往只能解决局部问题,因此只好"另起炉灶",进行重构。

重构拆译要求在准确地领会、把握原文的基础上,打破原文的结构,灵活自如地表达出原文的信息、含义。例如：

（1）The company's top executives all are refugees from the country's bureaucratic and underfinanced state research sector.

该公司的高层管理人员都来自该国的国家研究机构。这些机构不仅充满官僚主义气息，而且研究经费不足，他们很难在那里待下去。

（2）It is well said, in every sense, that a man's religion is the chief fact with regard to him.

有人说，看一个人，主要是看他的宗教信仰。这个说法无论在任何意义上都是恰当的。

（3）Lulled by the gentle motion and soothed by the rippling music of the waves the babies soon fell asleep.

船儿轻轻摇荡，波声潺潺悦耳，孩子们不久就睡着了。

佳译描红

以下段落选自史沫特莱的《伟大的道路》，请先通读再翻译，特别注意画线的句子。再与参考译文进行比较。

The Quest

Taking the train, the two friends arrived in Berlin in late October 1922, and went directly to the address of Chou En-lai. Would this man receive them as fellow countrymen, or would he treat them with cold suspicion and question them cautiously about their past careers as militarists? Chu Teh remembered his age. He was thirty-six, his youth had passed like a screaming eagle, leaving him old and disillusioned.

When Chou En-lai's door opened they saw a slender man of more than average height with gleaming eyes and a face so striking that it bordered on the beautiful. Yet it was a manly face, serious and intelligent, and Chu judged him to be in his middle twenties.

Chou was a quiet and thoughtful man, even a little shy as he welcomed his visitors, urged them to be seated and to tell how he could help them.

Ignoring the chair offered him, Chu Teh stood squarely before this youth more than ten years his junior and in a level voice told him who he was, what he had done in the past, how he had fled from Yunnan, talked with Sun Yat-sen, been repulsed by Chen Tu-hsiu in Shanghai, and had come to Europe to find a new way of life for himself and a new revolutionary road for China.

As he talked Chou En-lai stood facing him, his head a little to one side as was his habit, listening intently until the story was told, and then questioning him.

When both visitors had told their stories, Chou smiled a little, said he would help them find rooms, and arrange for them to join the Berlin Communist group as candidates until their application had been sent to China and an answer received. When the reply came a few months later they were enrolled as full members, but Chu's membership was kept a secret from outsiders.

(from Agnes Smedley: *The Great Road*)

【参考译文】

探 索

他们两个人坐火车于一九二二年十月下旬到达柏林,立即去了周恩来的住处。这个人会不会像同胞手足一样接待他们呢?会不会疑虑重重,详细询问他们在军阀时代的经历呢?朱德想起自己的年龄,36岁了,青春转瞬即逝,使他感到衰老和失望。

周恩来的房门打开时,他们看到的是一个身材修长,比普通人略高一点的人,两眼炯炯有神,面貌很引人注意,称得上是清秀。然而那是个男子汉的面庞,严肃而聪颖,朱德看他大概是二十五六岁的年龄。

周恩来举止优雅,待人体贴,在招呼他们坐下,询问他们有何见教的时候,甚至还有些腼腆。

朱德顾不得拉过来的椅子,端端正正地站在这个比他年轻十几岁的青年面前,用平稳的语调,说明自己的身份和经历:他怎样逃出云南,怎样会见孙中山,怎样在上海被陈独秀拒绝,怎样为了寻求自己新的生活方式和中国新的革命道路而来到欧洲。

他娓娓而谈,周恩来就站在他面前,习惯地侧着头,一直听到朱德把话说完,才提出问题。

两位来客把经历说完后,周恩来微笑着说,他可以帮他们找到住的地方,替他们办理加入党在柏林的支部的手续,在入党申请书寄往中国而尚未批准之前,暂作候补党员。过了几个月,回信来了,两人都被吸收为正式党员,但朱德的党籍对外界保密。

(选自梅念译:《伟大的道路》)

第五节　锁定行踪：定语从句的翻译

> **课前活动**

读下列短文,谈谈其中定语从句的翻译技巧。

Sand or Stone

A story tells that two friends were walking through the desert. In a specific point of the journey they had an argument, and one friend slapped the other one in the face.

The one who got slapped was hurt, but without saying anything, he wrote in the sand: TODAY MY BEST FRIEND SLAPPED ME IN THE FACE.

They kept on walking until they found an oasis, where they decided to take a bath. The one who had been slapped got stuck in the mire and started drowning, but the friend saved him. After he recovered from the fright, he wrote on a stone: TODAY MY BEST FRIEND SAVED MY LIFE.

The friend who had slapped and saved his best friend asked him, "After I hurt you, you wrote in the sand and now, you write on a stone, why?"

The other friend replied: "When someone hurts us we should write it down in sand where winds of forgiveness can erase it away. But, when someone does something good for us, we must engrave it in stone where no wind can ever erase it."

LEARN TO WRITE IN THE SAND.

写在沙子和石头上的话

有这样一则故事,两个朋友徒步穿行沙漠。旅行途中,他们发生了争执。其中一个人打了另一个人一记耳光。

被打耳光的那个人很伤心,但他沉默不语,只在沙地上写道:"今天,我最好的朋友打了我一耳光。"

他们继续前行,终于发现了一片绿洲。于是,他们决定洗个澡。结果,被打的那个人陷入了泥潭,眼看就要淹死了,幸好他的朋友救了他。惊魂甫定,他在一块石头上刻道:"今天,我最好的朋友救了我的命。"

打他耳光又救了他的那个朋友问道:"我打了你以后,你在沙子上写字;现在你又在石头上刻字。这是为什么呢?"

朋友回答道:"受到伤害时,我们应把它记在沙子上,这样,宽恕之风就能把它抚平。受人恩惠时,我们应把它刻在石头上,这样,没有什么能将他抹掉。"

学会在沙子上写字吧。

理论与技巧

英语是形合语言,其句式的扩展主要依靠各种非谓语结构及各种从句的使用。从句的类别较多,有主语从句、宾语从句、定语从句、状语从句、同位语从句等,大部分翻译时只需按拆分法翻译就可以了,不需要特别的翻译技巧。而其中定语从句的翻译由于其变数较多而成为这部分的一个重点。在汉语中,定语常位于所修饰的名词之前,而且不宜过长。与之相比,英语定语从句的位置则相对灵活,除了起修饰、限制作用以外,还可起补充说明等作用,逻辑上有时还可表示原因、条件、目的、结果等不同意义。定语从句的具体翻译技巧如下:

一、前置法

英语定语从句译为"……的"定语词组,置于所修饰词之前。例如:

A screwdriver is a tool which tightens or loosens screws.

螺丝刀是一种能拧紧或拆卸螺丝的工具。

二、后置法

定语从句较长时,如译成前置定语不符合汉语的表达习惯,可将其译成后置的分句。

1. 重复先行词

I told this news to Mary, who told it to her mother.

我把这个消息告诉了玛丽,玛丽又告诉了她妈妈。

2. 省略先行词

He saw in front that haggard white-haired old woman, whose teary eyes were filled with agony.

他看见前面那个憔悴的白发老妇人,眼睛里含着泪光,流露出痛苦的神情。

3. 关系代词译成人称代词

Wine was thicker than blood to the Mondavi brothers, who feuded bitterly over control of the family business, Charlskrug Winery.

对于蒙大维兄弟来说,"酒浓于血"。他们为争夺查尔斯·库勒格酿酒厂这份家业而结怨成仇。

4. 代词"这"指代整个句子

当关系代词指代整个句子时,可将关系代词译成指示代词"这"。例如:

China grows increasingly prosperous and strong, which is the key to the happiness of all of us.

中国更加繁荣强大,这是我们所有人福祉之关键所在。

三、融合法

英语中的 There be 句型和 It be 结构汉译时常用此译法,即将英语主语压缩成汉语词组做主语,将定语从句压缩成谓语。

There are many people in the city who really long for the country life.
城里许多人很渴望过乡村生活。

四、译成状语从句

英语中一些定语从句表示原因、条件、目的、结果等不同意义,即兼有状语的功能。在翻译这类定语从句时,要根据其实际含义恰当处理。例如:

(1) Many universities have "closed circuit" television equipments that will telecastlectures and demonstrations to hundreds of students in different classrooms.

许多大学都配备了"闭路"电视设备,以便为各个教室成百上千个学生进行电视讲授和演示。

(2) An electrical current begins to follow through a coil, which is connected across a charged capacitor.

如果把一个线圈接在已充电的电容器上,电流就开始流过它。

佳译描红

以下文字选自罗素的《记忆中的肖像》。请先通读,再翻译。特别注意画线句子的翻译。

Some old people are oppressed by the fear of death. In the young there is a justification for this feeling. <u>Young men who have reason to fear that they will be killed in battle may justifiably feel bitter in the thought that they have been cheated of the best things that life has to offer.</u> But in an old man who has known human joys and sorrows, and has achieved whatever work it was in him to do, the fear of death is somewhat abject and ignoble. The best way to overcome it—so at least it seems to me—is to make your interests gradually wider and more impersonal, until bit by bit the walls of the ego recede, and your life becomes increasingly merged in the universal life. An individual human existence should be like a river—small at first, narrowly contained within its banks, and rushing passionately past boulders and over waterfalls. Gradually the river grows wider, the banks recede, the waters flow more quietly, and in the end, without any visible break, they become merged in the sea, and painlessly lose their individual being. <u>The man who, in old age, can see his life in this way, will not suffer from the fear of death, since the things he cares for will continue.</u> And if, with the decay of vitality, weariness increases, the thought of rest will be not unwelcome. I should wish to die while still at work, knowing that others will carry on what I can no longer do, and content in the thought that what was possible has been done.

(from Bertrand Russell: *Portraits from Memory*)

【参考译文】

有些老年人因怕死而惶惶不安。年轻人有这种情绪是情有可原的。如果青年人由于某种原因认为自己有可能在战斗中死去,想到生活所能提供的最美好的东西自己全都无法享受,觉得受了骗,因而感到痛苦,这是无可指责的。但是对老年人来说,他经历了人生的酸甜苦辣,自己能做的事情都做到了,怕死就未免有些可鄙,有些不光彩了。要克服这种怕死的念头,最好的办法——至少在我看来——就是逐渐使自己关心更多的事情,关心那些不跟自己直接有关的事情,到后来,自我的壁垒就会慢慢消退,个人的生活也就越来越和宇宙的生命融合在一起了。人生好比一条河——开头河身狭小,夹在两岸之间,接着河水奔腾咆哮,流过巨石,飞下悬崖。后来河面逐渐展宽,两岸离得越来越远,河水也流得较为平缓,最后流进大海,与海水浑然一体,看不出任何界线,从而结束其单独存在的那一段历程,但毫无痛苦之感。如果一个人到了老年能够这样看待自己的一生,他就不会怕死了,因为他所关心的一切将会继续下去。如果随着精力的衰退,日见倦怠,就会觉得长眠未尝不是一件好事。我就希望在工作时死去,知道自己不再能做的事有人会继续做下去,并且怀着满意的心情想到,自己能做的事都已做到了。

(译自罗素《记忆中的肖像》)

第六节　谁主沉浮：汉英翻译之"主语的选择"

课前活动

分析下列句子的主谓结构,再将其译为英语。
(1) 这件事你不用操心。
(2) 全市都在兴建新的住宅。
(3) 发明计算机是人类历史上的一大奇迹。
(4) 应当强调(emphasize)指出,激光并不是一种能源。
(5) 一见到他我就恶心。
(6) 人生也许就是不断地放下,然而令人痛心的是,我都没能好好地与他们道别。(《少年派的奇幻漂流》)

All of life is an act of letting go, but _____.

理论与技巧

前面谈到过,汉文化重意念,句子建构在意念主轴上,而非结构上。从上面的例子可以看出,汉语和英语的句式差异,有相当一部分表现在主语上。在汉语中,没有主语,或主语不明显的句子仍然可以成立。而在英语里,没有主语的句子是例外情况。主语是整个英语句子中不可或缺的部分,它决定谓语的形态,由此构成了 SV(主语(subject)＋谓语(predicate))结构——英语句法构架的核心。

英语的 SV 结构要求主语与谓语在语义和逻辑关系上必须保持一致。而汉语中,句子的主语不一定是谓语动词的逻辑施动者,在很多情况下,二者是"主题"(topic)和"述题"(comment)的关系。

为了更好地理解什么是汉语的"主题＋述题"结构,请看以下例子:
(1) 各类书籍买了整整一书包。
(2) 两块钱一下子就花光了。

"各类书籍"并没有做出"买"的动作,"两块钱"也不会自己去"花"。正如赵元任先生所说:"在汉语中主语和谓语间的语法关系与其说是施事和动作的关系,不如说是话题和说明的关系。"主题(或称"话题")出现在汉语句子的开头部分,述题通常是"新的信息",用于对"话题"发表评论或说明。

"主题＋述题"结构反映了这样的思维过程:当讲话人想到一件事物或一个人时,往往将其脱口而出,然后再考虑如何对其进行评论和解释。这种句子在英语口语中虽然也存在,但并不普遍。

既然汉语的主语可以是一个"话题",名词性事物自然可以成为"话题",动词性、形容词性、数词性事物也可以成为"话题"。因此汉语的主语结构形式多种多样,有较强的词类兼容性。而英语的主语必须具有名词性。

了解了汉英在主语上的差异,就找到了汉英翻译的突破口。即:在汉译英时,译者必须首先为译句选择一个合适的主语,将原文中不明确的主语予以明确化。一旦主语确定下来,句子就"六神有主"了。具体有以下几种处理方法。

一、汉语中的"主题＋述题"结构译为英语中的主谓结构

例如:

(1) 你的提议(主题)我一定会认真考虑(说明部分)。

I'm(主语)sure to give serious thoughts to your suggestion(谓语部分).

(2) 这件事(主题)我得保密(说明部分)。

I(主语)have to keep quiet about this(谓语部分).

二、改变原句主语

如果原句中的主语并不适合在译句中做主语,译者便需为译句另外物色一个主语,使之符合英语的行文要求和习惯。例如:

(1) 故宫耗时14年,整个工程于1420年结束。

The construction of the Forbidden City took 14 years, and was finished in 1420.

(2) 这种水泵的主要特点是操作方便。

This pump is chiefly characterized by its simple operation.

另外,汉语比较注重主体思维,往往注重"什么人怎么了",因而,在主语位置上的常常是人或有生命的动物。英语则比较注重客体思维,叙事着眼点为"什么事发生在什么人身上",因此较多用非人称的物体或是抽象概念来充当句子的主语。基于这一差异,译者在翻译时应对主语进行相应的转换。例如:

(3) 一看到米粉,我就想起了我的家乡。

The sight of the rice noodles reminded me of my hometown.

(4) 听到这个好消息时,我高兴得一句话也说不出来。

The overwhelming happiness over the good news left me speechless.

(5) 又过了几个月,我看见他们手上戴了结婚戒指。可是他们不像以前那样健谈了,她在看书,他在看报。(胡文:《爱情故事》)

Months later, ring appeared glistening on their fingers but chatting became fewer for it was replaced by reading, one with a book and the other a newspaper.

三、汉语无主句译为英语主谓结构

当遇到没有主语的句子时,要仔细分析句子的结构和含义,为其选择一个合适的主语。例如:

(1) 历史上,由于长江不断改道,在武汉地区形成了众多的湖泊。

分析汉语原文,正是"长江不断改道"致使"众多的湖泊"形成,故选用"长江不断改道"作主语。

The constant change of the course of the Changjiang River in history helped form a great many lakes in the areas around Wuhan.

(2) 弄得不好,就会前功尽弃。

If things are not properly handled, our labour will be totally lost.

英语中即使是在谈论"天气"等比较抽象的事物时,也会用一个抽象的主语"it"。例如:

(3) 上海有好几年没下雪了。

It hasn't snowed for years here in Shanghai.

当然,虽然英汉两种语言在句法结构上存在很多差异,但相似或共同之处也很多。和英语一样,汉语中也存在着大量的主谓结构,这时原句中的主语也可以直接转换为英语译句中的主语。例如:

(4) 师生间的互动性以及学生之间的互动性也是学习过程的重要组成方面。

Instructor-student interactivity as well as student-student interactivity is also an important part of the learning process.

翻译视听

电影片段:《武状元苏乞儿》英文版
King of Beggars

苏灿:螳螂拳?像模像样的。音乐!

Look at you, you must be joking. Music! (暗讽转换为明讥)

苏灿:螳螂怎么打得过老虎?况且还有一只鹤。

A mantis can beat a tiger? Plus, I've got a hawk. (增加主语)

僧格林沁:虎鹤双形我也会。 ("主题+述题"结构)

(1) _____. (主谓结构)

赵无极:年轻人不知天高地厚。

(2) _____. (主语转换,正反转换)

苏父:哪个混蛋欺负我的儿子,我就毙了他。

Who are there bullying my son? I'll make him a hamburger. (译为英语习

语）

赵无极：王爷的令牌你也敢抢？抓起来！

So you steal a lord's seal? Arrest him! （"主题＋述题"转为主谓结构）

师爷：知法犯法，该当何罪？ （原句为无主句）

(3) I'm the governor of Canton. _____.（译文增加主语）

苏父：我身为广州将军，当然要把你们这些害群之马抓起来。

(4) _____. （人称主语转换为非人称主语）

赵无极：根据大清律例，任何人不束辫子一定要问斩。

According to Qing law, (5) _____. （主语转换，加连词）

老板：好了好了，别闹了。大家玩得这么开心就算了吧，苏将军。

Now wait a minute. This joke has gone far enough, gentlemen. （主语转换）

师爷：这个人惹不起，见好就收吧。

Leave this guy. He could be a bomber. （转换为祈使句）

师妹：这些酒菜里都下好了断肠散。 （"主题＋述题"结构）

(6) _____. （主谓结构）

长老：这个仇我们今天可以报了。 （"主题＋述题"结构）

(7) _____. （主谓结构）

苏灿：我果然没选错人。

(8) _____. （主语转换）

苏灿：我是真心要娶如霜姑娘为妻，若有半句假话，天打雷劈。

(9) _____. （中文成语转换为英语常用语，增加主语）

苏灿：因为中状元对我来说，易如反掌。

(10) _____. （主语翻译成不定式结构）

佳译描红

请把这些汉语名言先译为英语，再看看参考译文。注意主语的处理技巧。

(1) 欲穷千里目，更上一层楼。

(2) 有朋自远方来，不亦乐乎。

(3) 海内存知己，天涯若比邻。

(4) 举头望明月，低头思故乡。

(5) 学如逆水行舟，不进则退。

(6) 不登高山，不知天之厚也；不临深渊，不知地之厚也。

(7) 俱往矣,数风流人物,还看今朝。

(8) 顺天者存,逆天者亡。

【参考译文】

(1) Go further up one flight of stairs, and you'll widen your view a thousand li.

(2) It is such a delight to have friends coming from afar.

(3) If you have friends who know your heart, distance cannot keep you apart.

(4) Looking up, I find the moon bright; bowing, in homesickness I'm drowned.

(5) Learning is like rowing upstream: not to advance is to drop back.

(6) One can never be aware of the height of the sky or the depth of the earth, if he does not climb up a high mountain or look down into a deep abyss.

(7) All are past and gone; we look to this age for truly great men.

(8) Those who follow the Heaven's law will survive; those who go against it will perish.

第七节 一一到位：汉英翻译之"谓语的处理"

课前活动

试将以下电影台词译为英语：
（1）若有再提投降者，等同此桌！（《赤壁》）
（2）我们中国人习惯把姓放在前面，把名放在后面，表示对祖先的尊重。（《阮玲玉》）

理论与技巧

英语句子中，主谓结构就像一棵树的主干。只有当主谓确定后，"其他成分才可以像枝叶一样依附于它们而存在，这样，一个句子便可以成立并表达完整的意义。"（陈宏薇，1998）汉译英时，首先要确定好主语和选择好中心谓语。主谓定位是汉英翻译最重要的一步。

选择谓语时要注意汉语和英语在谓语上的差异：一个汉语句子中，往往出现多个动词，而英语句子则只注重一个中心谓语（并列谓语动词除外）。因此汉译英时要尽量做到"谓语最小化"，以符合英语的表达习惯。汉译英时谓语处理的具体技巧和注意事项如下。

一、选择谓语动词

1. 原句有多个动词时，选择主要动词做谓语

汉语的动词没有形态标志，可以在一个句子里连续使用，而英语的动词被赋予了严谨的形态，除谓语动词外，句子中的其他动词必须使用非谓语形态。因此在将汉语译成英语时，如果存在多个动词，要首先确定谓语动词。

汉语句子大量使用动词的情况，主要出现在两种句型里："连动式"和"兼语式"。

（1）连动式：暑假里她乘火车到西安去参观。

在这个句子中，"乘""到""去""参观"都是由主语"她"连续发出的几个动作，它们按时间的先后顺序排列，构成连动式。

（2）兼语式：她责备孩子迟迟不回家。

在这个句子中，"责备孩子"是动宾词组，"孩子"既是前面"她"的宾语，又是后面"不回家"的主语，兼任两个句子成分，故称"兼语式"。

选择谓语动词时,要先对句子结构进行分析,确定主次。在第一个句子里,"乘火车"是方式,"参观"是目的。可选择"去西安"做谓语动词。第二个句子里,"责备"显然是主要动作,"孩子不回家"是受责备的原因。两个句子可分别译为:

(1) She went to Xi'an for a visit by train during the summer vocation.

(2) She reproached her child for staying out late.

2. 所选择的谓语应该与主语在逻辑上搭配得当

当我们选择句子的主语时,其实已经同时将谓语考虑进去了,因为英语中主语和谓语之间有很强的制约性。有学者对英语主谓结构做了一个比喻:英语的主语和谓语犹如两根柱子,而这两根"柱子"一定要有一根"梁"搭在它们上面。这个"梁"就是主谓一致的语法关系。汉英翻译时,要通盘考虑主语和谓语的选择,如果主谓不一致,就要对其中一个进行调整。

(1) 我们同敌人的斗争取得了一个又一个胜利。

误译:Our struggle against the enemy has won one victory after another.

英语强调主谓之间的逻辑关系,只有有生命的"人"才能"won victory"。

改译:We have won one victory after another in the struggle against the enemy.

再如:

(2) 他的英语讲得很好。

误译:His English speaks good.

改译:He speaks good English.

(3) 汉语部教汉语和中国文学课。

误译:The Chinese Program teaches courses of Chinese and Chinese Literature.

主语是"汉语部"时,英语中不能用原文中的"教"做谓语,应根据主谓一致的原则,选择更合适的动词作谓语。

改译:The Chinese Program offers courses of Chinese and Chinese Literature.

3. 所选择的谓语必须与宾语搭配得当

汉译英时,要"瞻前顾后",不仅考虑主谓一致,还要考虑动宾搭配,请看下面的例子:

谁来养活中国的问题,实际情况究竟怎样呢?看粮食,要看中国的农业;看农业,首先要看市场。

Then what are the facts about who is going to provide food for China? To know the food provision situation in China we have to take a full view of her agriculture, for which we should look at her market.

原文有四个动词"看",含义都不同。"看粮食"的意思是"了解"粮食产量和粮食供应的情况;"看农业"是指对农业作全面的了解;"看市场"指"观察市场的情况"。

4. 原文若含有被动意义,译文中应该用被动式做谓语

(1) 一切科技成就都是建立在理性思维的基础上的,没有理性思维就不可能有科学。

All scientific and technological achievements are founded on rational thinking, without which there would have been no science.

分析:"……是……的"是一种形式标志,含有这种形式标志的汉语在英译时往往可以用被动语态的形式做谓语。

(2) 两个物体一起摩擦时,电子便从一个物体转到另一个物体上。

When two objects are rubbed together, electrons are transferred from one object to the other.

分析:原文是主动形式,但含有被动意义,故译文用被动形式。

二、主谓确立后其他句子成分的安排

当英语句子里的主谓结构确立后,就要考虑其他成分的安排。只有所有成分安排合理有序,整个句子才能脉络分明,井然有序。

其他句子成分的安排,要着眼于整句意义的完整表达,处理好原文中其他以动词形式出现的成分与中心谓语动词的关系,并根据需要使用恰当的非谓语形式。例如:

(1) 得病以前,我受父母宠爱,在家中横行霸道。

Before I fell ill, I had been the bully under our roof owing to my doting parents.

分析:原句中出现几个动词短语:"得病""受宠爱""横行霸道"等。译文以 had been the bully 作为谓语,突出了信息中心,而"受父母宠爱"是"横行霸道"的原因,译为"owing to"引导的介词短语。

又如朱自清《荷塘月色》中的一个句子:

(2) 我悄悄地披了大衫,带上门出去。

Shrugging on an overcoat, quietly, I made my way out, closing the door behind me. (朱纯深译)

I quietly slipped on a long gown, and walked out leaving the door on the latch. (杨宪益译)

两位翻译家虽然处理方式略有不同,但因为恰当地选择了谓语,并确定了从属成分的形式,译文都达到了主次分明、重点突出的效果。

第二章 翻译技巧

课堂练习

下面几个句子的翻译有什么问题？如何改正？

(1) 四分卫把球夹在臂下冲过了门线。
注：四分卫(quarterback)是橄榄球赛中的助理球员。
Rushing across the goal-line, the quarterback carried the ball under his arm.

(2) 你的教学科研取得了很大的进步。
Your teaching and research has made great progress.

(3) 现在人们的生活离不开电视。
Now people's life can't leave TV.

(4) 他的讲座不仅仅局限于教学法。
His lecture didn't confine only to teaching methods.

翻译视听

请先将以下台词回译为英语，再观看电影片段，比较台词和你的译文。

《功夫熊猫》(Kung fu Panda)

(1) 阿宝：功夫需要勤修苦练，对不对？你胳膊酸不酸？

_____

(2) 灵鹤：我今天又累又失望，所以……

_____

(3) 阿宝：我今天的糟糕表现恐怕是功夫史上之最了。也是中国历史之最，糟糕历史之最！

_____
_____

佳译赏析

1、《初到中国旅游可到哪些地方》（摘选）
Travel Tips for First-Time China Tourists（Excerpt）

问：第一次到中国旅游，应当先去哪些地方？
答：这首先要看您能安排多少时间。一般地说，第一次到中国应当先到北京、上海、西安等地。
Q: Which cities are preferable for visitors on their first trip to China?

A: It depends on how long they stay in China. Generally speaking, though, most foreign visitors choose to visit cities like Beijing, Shanghai and Xi'an on their first trip to China.

这是一篇以问答的形式对外介绍中国风光名胜的文章。译者根据语言和文化的差异,对主语和谓语都做了恰当的处理。

原文问句里没有主语,因为在汉语里,既然主语是外国游客这一点是不言而喻的,就可以不说出来。英语里则要补充上去。

原文问句和答句里都有的"应当"一词,在译文中得到不同处理。首先,在英语表达里,到哪里去旅游,不是"应不应当"的问题,而是"哪个选择更好",因此问句中用 preferable 一词。在答句里,"应当"一词则没有译出。英语文化强调阐述客观事实,因此只告知"多数游客会去的地方",将选择权留给对方。

上海是中国最大城市,在这里选购物品最合适,上海品种繁多的小吃、糕点和手工艺品、纺织品,会使您感到满意。离上海仅有几小时路程的苏州和杭州,是中国园林艺术的代表,被人称为"天堂"。

Shanghai, a shopping center for best buys, is the largest city in China. Tourists will find it difficult to make a choice from a good variety of snacks and cakes to a multiplicity of handicrafts and textiles. Neighbouring Suzhou and Hangzhou, only a couple of hours away from Shanghai by train or by car, are two garden cities that embody the essence of Chinese gardening architecture. For this reason, both of them are considered by the Chinese to be "paradise on earth".

注意译文对句子主干和从属成分的处理。"上海是中国最大城市"作为主句;而"在这里选购物品最合适",在汉语中是一个分句,在英语里则处理为一个名词性词组,紧跟在 Shanghai 后面做同位语。这种将汉语的分句译为词组的方法,是汉英句式转换的常用技巧,这样就精简了译文中的谓语,符合英文的表达习惯,有人称之为"谓语最小化"原则。对"苏州"和"杭州"的介绍,在汉语里只有一个句子,译者通过对句内逻辑关系的分析,增加了 for this reason 这个连接性词组,译为两个句子,更加清楚明了。

这一段的翻译还涉及汉语长句翻译的切分和合并的问题,有关内容在下一章将得到更详尽的阐述。

2. 孔乙己便涨红了脸,额上的青筋条条绽出,争辩道,"窃书不能算偷……窃书!……读书人的事,能算偷么?"(鲁迅:《孔乙己》)

At that Kong Yiji would flush, the veins on his forehead standing out as he protested, "Taking books can't be counted as stealing… Taking books… for a scholar… can't be counted as stealing."(杨宪益、戴乃迭译)

句式的处理:原文有两个主语,"孔乙己"和"额上的青筋",但从全句语义来看,显然孔乙己才是全句叙述的主体,应该作为句子的主语。主语确定后,主语的两个动作"涨红了脸"和"争辩",前者作为谓语,后者以伴随状语从句的形式表达,显得层次分明。而"额上的青筋条条绽出"这个句子,虽然同样是表现孔乙己的神态,但其主语跟全句主语不一致,故译为自带主语的独立主格结构。

译文的连贯性:句子开头介词短语 at that(that 指代前文中酒店客人嘲笑孔乙己的话)的使用,自然而然承接上文。as 引导状语从句,全句一气呵成,顺达流畅。

词义的选择:在孔乙己的口里,"偷"变成了文绉绉的"窃",译文里用了正大光明的词"take",读来也有幽默的感觉。只是译文未能像汉语那样,形象地传达出孔乙己的书呆子形象,这只能说是翻译中无法找到完全对应词汇的遗憾。

3. 唐小姐妩媚端正的圆脸,有两个浅酒窝。天生着一般女人要花钱费时、调脂和粉来仿造的好脸色,新鲜得使人忘记口渴而又觉得嘴馋,仿佛是好水果。(钱钟书:《围城》)

On Miss Tang's charming, well-proportioned, round face were two shallow dimples; one look at the fresh and natural complexion, which most girls would have had to spend time and money to imitate, was enough to make one drool and forget his thirst, as though her skin were a piece of delicious fruit. (Jeanne Kelly, Nathan Mao 译)

原文有两个句子。第一句的意思,可以理解为"唐小姐长着妩媚端正的圆脸",而且"有两个浅酒窝",但是这样的话,就要翻译成 and 连接的两个并列谓语,显得拖沓。译文则要紧凑得多,用"浅酒窝"做主语,而将前一句变成状语,即"浅酒窝"长在"妩媚端正的圆脸"上。倒装句式的使用,将信息重量放在句子末端,译文轻灵生动。

第二句主语的确定尤其困难。但分析全句语意,可以发现句子主要是强调唐小姐肤色给人美的感觉。译文利用英语中的非灵主语 look,从观察者的角度着眼,巧妙地将全句信息整合起来。可见主谓定位对整合语意起着至关重要的作用。

第八节　聚散有时：汉英翻译之"流水长句的翻译"

> **课前活动**

想一想：为什么汉语长句叫"流水句"？你还能想出其他形象的称谓吗？

> **理论与技巧**

跟英语中以主谓结构为核心的复合长句不同，汉语中的长句常以"流水句"的形式出现。只要句子围绕一个相关话题展开，就可以一口气说下来，与话题相关的可能有几件事或者多个人，因此可以出现不同的主语和多个动词，中间似断似连，一逗到底，最后才以句号结束。

翻译这种由多层分句组成的汉语长句时，需要"先分后合"，即先按照句子的逻辑关系，将长句切分为几个意群，在此基础上，再将一个意群内的分句加以合并。这样得到一组主次分明、层次清晰的英语句子。

一、汉语长句的切分

逻辑关系是切分的重要依据。由于汉语的断句是句随意止，流水句有时铺排得很开，再加上汉语长句缺乏形式标记，所以在切分时，首先是理清原文各层意义之间的逻辑关系。

除了考虑逻辑关系的合理性，还要考虑切分是否有可操作性及是否适度。适度指切分粗细适度；可操作性主要指切开后，便于表达。

以下为《红楼梦》中一个长句的两个英译版本，请比较译者的不同切分方式。

这里宝玉悲恸了一会，忽然抬头不见了黛玉，便知黛玉看见他躲开了，自己也觉得无味，抖抖土起来，下山寻归旧路，往怡红院来。（《红楼梦》）

When Baoyu recovered sufficiently to look up, she had gone, obviously to avoid him. Getting up rather sheepishly, he dusted off his clothes and walked down the hill to make his way back again to Happy Red Court. （杨宪益、戴乃迭译）

By the time Baoyu's weeping was over, Daiyu was no longer there. He realized that she must have seen him and have gone away in order to avoid him. Feeling rather foolish, he rose to his feet and brushed the earth from his clothes. Then he descended from the rockery and began to retrace his steps in the direction of Green Delights. (大卫·霍克斯译)

从两个不同的译版可以看出:切分粗细的不同,往往会影响到作品的风格。杨宪益、戴乃迭版将原文切成两个意群,翻译成两个英文句子,译文干练紧凑。大卫·霍克斯的译文则将原文切分为四个意群,行文细致绵密。

二、切分后短句的合并

1. 汉语短句合并的必要性

长句切分后,一个意群里的一组短句需要合并为英语里的一个句子,即英语的复合句。以朱自清《背影》的翻译为例:

我们过了江,进了车站。我买票,他忙着照看行李。

译文一:We crossed the River. Then we entered the station. I bought the ticket, and father saw to my luggage.

译文二:We crossed the Yangtze and arrived at the station, where I bought a ticket while he saw to my luggage.

译文一按汉语思维习惯译为几个小短句,仅用 and 加以连接;译文二则对短句加以合并。表达效果之优劣判然分明。

2. 合理处理主句与从属成分的关系

可是,在一组汉语短句中,往往有几个动词,有时还有几个主语,选择哪一组作为主句的主、谓语?

首先是要透彻理解原文,吃透原作者的写作意图以及原文的逻辑关系。选择主语和谓语时要突出重点,逻辑合理,同时也要兼顾是否便于表达。

同样以前面《红楼梦》中长句为例,虽然杨宪益和大卫·霍克斯的译版切分粗细不同,但他们都不约而同地选择了以"黛玉离开"和"宝玉站起身"为主要动词。这是当时最重要的两个事件,当事人的感受则处理为从属成分。黛玉离开的原因,两个版本中均处理为表示目的的不定式 to avoid him;宝玉站起时的感受,杨版中用副词 sheepishly 来传达,霍克斯版则用分词 feeling rather foolish 来表达。

3. 合理增加衔接手段

雨是最寻常的,一下就是三两天。可别恼,看,像牛毛,像花针,像细丝,密密地斜织着,人家屋顶上全笼着一层薄烟。(朱自清:《春》)

汉语往往不用关联词,也能让读者意会到词与词、句与句之间的联系。看看上面这段文字里省略了哪些"不言而喻"的衔接手段吧:

雨是最寻常的,一下就是三两天。(不过)可别恼,看,(它)像牛毛,像花针,像细丝,密密地斜织着,(以至于)人家屋顶上全笼着一层薄烟。

在英语中,关联词是必不可少的,否则便难以理解。试将中文与此段英文译文比较:

Rain is nothing unusual now, and often lasts two to three days. Never get annoyed! Look, could it be ox hair, or needles, or thin threads instead? Those thin threads simply weave sideways, so densely that a thin mist pervades over all the house-tops.

除了关联词,代词的指代功能也可以看作一种形式衔接手段。汉语中省略代词是常有的事,而英语中却很少省略。比如,"像牛毛"可以不用主语,英文中 it 却是不能少的。

4. 必要时可调整语序或删减原文

如果汉语长句容量很大,构成了一个较长的语篇,翻译时要有全局观念。可根据英语习惯调整语序。另外,汉语译为英语时,篇幅一般比原文长,读起来就不够简洁,所以可适当删减以突出重点。而且,英语忌重复,汉语原文中重复的地方,也可删减。从整体效果上来说,这样更忠实于原文。

以下例子来自匡佩华和曹珊翻译的《牡丹亭》,汉语部分由陈美林根据明朝汤显祖的原著改编而成。

①不觉冬去春来,/②久困思动,/③今日醒来,阳光照屋,精神为之一振,/④扔在屋角的包袱一直未曾打开,(趁天气晴朗,)一把拎了过来,抖出冬天换下的衣裳,/⑤上面尚有点点雨渍雪痕,便将它摊在窗前晒起。

①Before very long, winter passed and spring arrived. ③One day when Liu Mengmei woke up, he was pleased to find that the room full of sunshine. ②He had lain on the bed for a long time and now found it better to get up and move around. ④He jumped up and took up the bundle which he had thrown in the corner of the room many days ago. ⑤His winter clothes still had stains of rain and snow and he hung them up by the window to dry.

分析:第二句"久困思动"在英文中移到了第三句后面,跟后面的 jumped up and took up the bundle 衔接更紧;由于天气情况前面已有交代,"趁天气晴朗"在英文中删掉了,并未翻译出来。

佳译赏析

我的故事,从 1950 年 1 月 1 日讲起。

在此之前两年多的时间里,我在阴曹地府里受尽了人间难以想象的酷刑。每次提审,我都会鸣冤叫屈。我的声音悲壮凄凉,传播到阎罗大殿的每个角落,激发出重重叠叠的回声。我身受酷刑而绝不改悔,挣得了一个硬汉子的名声。我知道许多鬼卒对我暗中钦佩,我也知道阎王老子对我不胜厌烦。为了让我认罪服输,他们使出了地狱酷刑中最凶毒的一招,将我扔到沸腾的油锅里,翻来覆去,像炸鸡一样炸了半个时辰,痛苦之状,难以言表。鬼卒还用叉子把我叉起来,高高举着,一步步走上通往大殿的台阶。两边的鬼卒撮口吹哨,如同成群的吸血蝙蝠鸣叫。我的身体滴油浙沥,落在台阶上,冒出一簇簇黄烟……鬼卒小心翼翼地将我安放在阎罗殿前的青石板上,跪下向阎王报告:"大王,炸好了。"

——莫言《生死疲劳》

My story begins on January 1, 1950. ①In the two years prior to that, I suffered cruel torture such as no man can imagine in the bowels(内部) of hell. Every time I was brought before the court, I proclaimed(宣称) my innocence in solemn and moving, sad and miserable tones that penetrated(穿透)every crevice(缝隙) of Lord Yama's Audience Hall and rebounded in layered echoes. ②Not a word of repentance(悔过) escaped my lips though I was tortured cruelly, for which I gained the reputation of an iron man. ③I know I earned the unspoken respect of many of Yama's underworld attendants, but I also know that Lord Yama was sick and tired of me. So to force me to admit defeat, they subjected(使……遭受) me to the most sinister(令人毛骨悚然的)form of torture hell had to offer: they flung me into a vat(大缸) of boiling oil, in which I tumbled and turned and sizzled(发"呲呲"声) like a fried chicken for about an hour. Words cannot do justice to the agony experienced until an attendant speared me with a trident(三叉戟) and, holding me high, carried me up to the palace steps. He was joined by another attendant, one on either side, who screeched(发出尖叫声) like vampire bats as scalding(滚烫的) oil dripped from my body onto the Audience Hall steps, where it sputtered and produced puffs of yellow smoke. ④With care, they deposited me on a stone slab at the foot of the throne, and then bowed deeply.

"Great Lord," he announced, "he has been fried." ⑤

—*Life and Death Are Wearing Me Out* (translated by Howard Goldblatt)

【评析】

①原文"我的故事,从1950年1月1日讲起"中,主语是"我的故事",而动词是"讲",并不是严格的主谓关系。翻译成英文后,动词则选择了begin,与主语story构成主谓一致的逻辑关系。

②从"每次提审"到"回声",原文是两个句子。但译文利用英语里介词短语和定语从句的粘连作用,译为一个句子,连贯而有气势。

③原文从开头到这里,已经几次用了第一人称"我"做主语。译文在这里将主语换为非人称的 not a word of repentance,符合英文表达习惯,而且句式更有多样性。

④连贯性是故事讲述的基本要求。汉语利用连动式和兼语式的独特句式,一波一波将情节向前推进,读来有行云流水般的连贯感。而英文则主要通过连词和

介词的粘连作用来实现连贯。译者用 until 将"痛苦之状,难以言表"与后句连接起来;继而用代词 he 指代前面的 attendant 作为主语,引出第二个 attendant;而"我的身体滴油淅沥"的情况,则放在以 as 引导的伴随状语从句中,与前面的主要信息相连,达到声气相合,引领有序的连贯感。当然,由于文化的隔阂,这里译者对"鬼卒"的数量显然理解有误。

⑤原文"大王,炸好了。"汉语用时态助词来表示完成,而英文中用完成时态 he has been fried 来表达。时态的准确使用是初学汉英翻译者容易忽视的,要加以留意。

第三章

文体与翻译

第一节 严谨为先：科技翻译

一、科技英语的文体特征和语言特点

科技文献是对客观事物及其发展规律的描述，讲究实事求是、客观准确，这就赋予了科技英语客观、明确、严谨、规范、简洁的文体特征。体现在语言表达上，有以下几个主要特点。

1. 无灵名词做主语

科技文献报告的是自然规律或科技活动的结果，往往以讨论的客观对象为主语，因此频繁出现无灵名词（无生命体的名词）主语。注意无灵名词和有灵名词使用同一个动词做谓语时，意义是不一样的。例如：

(1) The engineering project promises well. （无灵名词做主语。）

这个工程项目大有希望。

(2) He promised us well.

他郑重地向我们承诺。

2. 被动语态

科技文章重视事实和推理，强调客观、准确。虽然人类参与了科技活动，但在很多情况下，不必提及人，因为过多使用第一、二人称会造成主观臆断的印象。应尽量采用第三人称叙述，这就会大量用到被动语态。运用被动语态还避免了不必要的人称代词，使句子结构更紧凑。例如：

Attention must be paid to the working temperature of the machine.

而很少说：You must pay attention to the working temperature of the machine.

3. 长难句

为了明确陈述有关事物的内在特征和相互联系，科技英语中常采用包含很多

从句的复合句,句子较长,结构较复杂。

Summary must be a condensed version of body of the report, written in language understandable by those members of mine management who may not be specialists in the field of rock testing, but who are nonetheless responsible for the work.

摘要必须是报告的编写本,要以矿山管理部门人员能够理解的语言编写;他们虽然负责岩石试验工作,但不是这方面的专家。

有时为了准确、简练,又常常使用非谓语动词(不定式、分词和动名词)及短语来代替从句。例如:

Vibrating objects produce sound waves, each vibration producing one sound wave.

振动着的物体产生声波,每一次振动产生一个声波。

另外,科技文献中所涉及的定义、定理、结论等抽象概念比一般文章要多,且其文体要求行文简洁、信息量大,因此科技英语中较多地使用名词和介词短语。例如:

The rotation of the earth on its own axis causes the change from day to night.

地球绕轴自转,引起昼夜的变化。

在这个句子里,名词化结构 the rotation of the earth on its own axis 使复合句简化成简单句,而且使表达的概念更加确切、严密。

4. 科技新词

由于科技发展日新月异,科技英语中往往含有大量新词汇。一般有以下构词方法:

(1) 通过前缀和后缀组成新词:英语中,一些词缀得到广泛使用,构成大量新词。如 electro-(电), bio-(生命、生物), carbo-(碳), thermo-(热), aero-(空气), hydro-(水、氢), -ite(矿物), -mania(热、狂)等。

(2) 通过词的组合构成新词:由两个或两个以上的旧词合成一个新词。如: moonwalk(月面行走), pulse-scaler(脉冲定标器)等。或取两个词的一部分,叠合生成新词,如 smog 由 smoke 和 fog(烟雾)部分叠合而成。

(3) 在特定科技领域里,一些英语词汇获得其常见意义之外的新含义。transmission 在无线电工程学中的词义是"发射""播送",在机械学中的词义是"转动""变速",在物理学中的词义是"透射",在医学中的涵义是"遗传",等等。power 更是一词多义的典型代表,仅在机械动力学一个专业中它的词义就有"力""电""电力""电源""动力""功率"等。

二、科技英语翻译的原则

科技英语翻译也要做到"信、达、雅"。"信"是指忠实、准确地传达原文的信息;

"达"是指清晰、易懂;科技翻译的"雅",则体现为简练、贴切。

对于科技英语翻译来说,准确性是最基本的要求。要注意原文理解准确、专业术语翻译准确。请看下面的例子:

There must be many kinds of thermometric materials, because we use many different thermometers.

原译:因为我们使用许多不同的温度计,所以必须有许多种测温物质。

译文令人费解,"测温物质"是早就客观存在的,怎么受温度计的影响呢?原因就在于译者对连词 because 的用法了解不全面,把原文以事实为根据的推理误解成了因果关系。

改译:我们使用的温度计有各式各样,由此不难想到,测温物质的种类一定很多。

对于科技翻译来说,清晰和简练也是重要的翻译标准。试比较以下各组例子:

(1) There is no time when the circulation of water doesn't take place.

译文一:没有时候水的循环不发生。

译文二:水循环无时不在进行。

(2) Very pure copper is needed for the wires used in electrical engineering, because quite small amounts of some impurities make copper a much poor conductor of electricity.

译文一:电工中应用的导线需要用很纯的铜来制造,因为相当少量的某种杂质就会使铜成为差得多的导电体。

译文二:电气导线需要很纯的铜,因为极少量的杂质都会使导电性能大大下降。

(3) Place a clean iron part in the solution of copper sulphate, and the part will be coated with red copper.

译文一:把一个干净的铁制件放在硫酸铜溶液中,它就会涂上一层紫铜。

译文二:把一洁净铁制件放入硫酸铜溶液,就会镀上一层紫铜。

以上各句,译文一虽然没有背离原文的意义,但含混冗长,造成理解困难,未能完成翻译任务。经过调整后,译文二行文符合清晰简洁的要求。

总之,翻译科技作品不像翻译文艺作品那样,需要在形象化的语言和修辞手段上花很大工夫,但要求概念清楚、逻辑正确、文字简练。

三、科技英语翻译基本方法

在翻译方法上,要处理好直译和意译的关系。直译读得通的,就不需意译。在文学、艺术等领域,因涉及不同文化和社会习俗而产生思想和语言表达的巨大差异,从而出现"不可译"问题。而在科技英语中这种情况不多。科技英语在行文方面,讲究确切、严密、简练,不会像文学语言那样大量使用修饰性和抒情性词语,句法也不会那样随意。这些都为直译提供了条件。更重要的是,科技英语讲求准确和严谨,直译可以最有效地保持原作者的写作意图和语言特点。比如:

It is when a gas is heated that its volume is increased.

正是当气体受热时它的体积才增大。(原文为强调句,译文也顺译为强调句。)

但是,毕竟英汉两种语言在词法和句法上都存在较大差异,如果过分拘泥于直译,未能有效使用翻译技巧,导致译文晦涩难懂,也就不能圆满地完成翻译任务。译者应本着科技翻译"忠实、通顺、简练"的标准,在直译优先的前提下,根据具体情况适当使用意译的方法。例如:

The average speed of all molecules remains the same so long as the temperature is constant.

只要温度不变,(全部)分子的总平均速度也就不变。(按照汉语习惯,将条件从句倒译在主句前面。)

四、科技英语翻译技巧

1. 无主句和被动语态的翻译

由于汉语中同样强调客观性,科技英语含被动语态的句子译为汉语时,在不违背汉语表达习惯的前提下,不一定要转换为主动语态。但要注意,汉语习惯略去"被"字,或用其他的字词代替。注意以下例句中被动语态的多种翻译方法。

The Bessemer process uses a furnace <u>called</u> a "converter". The outside of the converter <u>is made of</u> steel plates. The inside <u>is lined with</u> bricks. The converter <u>is tipped</u> onto its side and the charge of molten iron <u>is poured into</u> the top. Then the converter <u>is put upright</u> again. A blast of air is <u>blown</u> through holes in the base of the converter.

有一种高炉称为"转炉",采用酸性转炉法。转炉的外壳<u>由钢板制成</u>。内部<u>用耐火砖衬砌</u>。<u>把</u>转炉向一侧侧转后,从炉顶<u>把</u>铁水倒入炉中。<u>再把</u>炉子转回直立位置。从炉子底部的孔中<u>把</u>空气吹入炉中。

2. 长句翻译

拆译长句时,要注意理清逻辑关系。在词序安排上,科技英语翻译中的长句,尽量顺拆,以保持原文的逻辑和顺序,防止由于状语位置的不适当异动造成的表达错误,或者该强调的部分没得到应有的强调。例如:

(1) The hydrogen produced by electrolysis is nearly pure, though rather more expensive than that obtained by the thermal cracking process.

用电解法生产的氢几乎是纯氢,虽然比用热裂法制取的氢稍微昂贵一些。

原文强调的是电解氢的纯度高,从句仅仅起到补充说明的作用,因此译文尽量保留原有语序,将让步状语从句放在后面。

但是,当顺译不能很好表达原文含义或者不符合"通顺""简练"的要求时,就需要采取"倒译法"。

(2) A signal will be shown wherever anything wrong occurs with the control system.

无论控制系统什么地方发生故障,都会有信号发出。

长句翻译时,还应注意从句的处理。如翻译状语从句时,连词的翻译不要仅仅从字面上理解,when 不一定译成"当",if 不一定译成"如果",because 也不必都译为"因为",而应酌情进行转译或简化。例如:

(3) Where there is nothing in the path of the beam of light, nothing is seen.

如果光轨迹上没有东西,就什么也看不出来。

3. 科技术语的翻译

科技术语翻译的首要原则是"基于规范",科技术语的翻译往往已有约定俗成的规范说法。在翻译过程中,首先要借助各类国家标准、百科全书、权威著作、官方文件寻找最权威、最贴切的译法,并结合自己的翻译知识作出取舍。特别要留意词汇在不同学科领域的不同含义。注意以下各句中"power"一词的翻译:

(1) The fourth power of 2 is 16.

2 的 4 次方是 16。

(2) Aluminium has a combining power of three.

铝的化合价是三。

(3) The electronic microscope possesses very high resolving power compared with the optical microscope.

与光学显微镜相比,电子显微镜具有极高的分辨率。

对于尚没有规范翻译的新词,应认真分析其各个组成部分的含义,运用构词法知识和专业领域知识确定其词义。如在 fuel oil filter 中,前两个词 fuel 与 oil 结合较紧,成为一个意义单位(燃油),应译为"燃油过滤器",而在 aircraft gas turbine 中,后两个单词 gas 与 turbine 已紧密结合为一个意义单位(燃气轮机),整个词应译为"飞机燃气轮机"。

总之,要翻译好特定领域科技文章,必须做好功课,熟悉构词方法,阅读相关的中英文科技文献,必要时向专业人员请教,以保证翻译的准确、规范。

课堂练习

请比较以下句子的不同翻译版本,选出更好的一个,并说明理由:

(1) Action is equal to reaction, but it acts in a contrary direction.

a. 作用力与反作用力相等,但它们向相反的方向起作用。

b. 作用力与反作用力大小相等,方向相反。

(2) The engine has given a constantly good performance.

a. 这台发动机给出良好的工作性能。

b. 这台发动机一直工作良好。

(3) The dead-soft condition of aluminium foil is the one best suited for most packaging applications.

a. 铝箔极软，最适合于做大多数物品的包装材料。

b. 铝箔的极软状态是最适合于大多数包装用途的状态。

(4) In all such reactions we have the hydrogen in the acid replaced by the metal to form a salt.

a. 所有这类反应都是用金属置换酸中的氢，制成一种金属盐。

b. 在所有这些反应中，我们都是让酸中的氢被金属取代，从而生成了盐。

(5) Areturus is 200 million million miles away, and to feel its heat you would have to be able to feel the warmth of a candle from a distance of 5 miles.

a. 大角星在200万亿英里以外，若要感觉到它的热，你就要能感觉出5英里外一支蜡烛的热量。

b. 大角星距地球200万亿英里，只有你能觉出5英里外一支蜡烛燃烧的温度，才能感知它散发出的热量。

(6) The patient chair is adjustable in three dimensions and precisely controlled by a joystick mounted right in front of the microscope where doctors can easily reach and accurately adjust prior to operation.

a. 患者座椅可做三维调节，由一个操纵杆精确控制；该操纵杆安装于显微镜正前方医生伸手可及的位置，便于在术前做精确调节。

b. 可三维调节的患者座椅由一操纵杆精确控制于显微镜正前方，这正是医生所处的位置，术前医生在此对显微镜做精确调节。

第二节　光影世界：影视翻译

影视作品以其独特的魅力，已经成为跨越国界的艺术形式。但由于语言和文化隔阂，影视作品需要经过翻译才能更好地被其他语言的观众理解和欣赏。翻译质量对影视艺术效果的传递有着至关重要的作用。电影字幕翻译通常分为两类：为电影配音所做的翻译和为原声电影添加字幕的翻译。

一、影视字幕的特点

1）短时存在性

电影作品本身的特点决定了影视字幕语言的短时存在性。字幕与影片对话同步，往往一闪而过。因此，字幕翻译力求简洁。

2）空间局限性

影视字幕一般是出现在屏幕的底部，不能覆盖影视作品中的画面。字幕一般只有一行，最多不能超过两行，每行的字数也要受到屏幕宽度的限制。

3）音画配合性

在电影作品中，除了占主导地位的口头语言外，还包括影片中的背景音乐、肢体语言等，而且这些语言也不是相互孤立的，而是相互作用的，共同构成影片不可或缺的部分。

4）语言的通俗性和艺术性

影视语言以口语化的表达为主，往往有大量的体现本土文化特色的习语、俚语，多用双关等修辞手法，角色的个人语言风格明显，感情色彩强烈，有的还有强烈的幽默感。

二、影视字幕翻译的原则

影视字幕的以上特点，给翻译时兼顾"信、达、雅"三方面的翻译原则提出了难题。但根据电影艺术的特点，奈达的"功能对等原则"（又称"动态对等原则"）有助于解决三者之间的矛盾。影视欣赏的过程是一种审美体验过程，离开了观众的审美体验，影视作品的美学特质就得不到完整的体现。因此，电影字幕翻译必须以观众为中心。而奈达的"功能对等原则"强调的是，译本读者能以与源本读者相一致的方式去理解和欣赏作品。在电影字幕翻译中，如果目标语言观众对电影的理解和欣赏，及其观看电影后的感受和反应与原版电影的观众达到一致，翻译的目的就达到了。

根据这一原则，我们在翻译过程中，应以观众为中心，充分考虑到观众的文化背景和审美方式,根据具体情况,灵活使用各种翻译策略和技巧,实现两种语言转换结果的动态对等。

三、影视字幕翻译的策略

1. 归化和异化

电影字幕中常常携带丰富的文化内容,但是可能给国外观众陌生感,甚至完全不能理解。为了使有译入语文化背景的观众能够轻松自然地欣赏国外电影,字幕翻译中常常使用归化的翻译方法。

如在电影《让子弹飞》中的一段对话:

——前汤师爷:"马县长此番风度,正好比'大风起兮云飞扬!'"(Governor, with your style and poise, you remind me of a modern-day Robin Hood!)

——马夫人:"屁!"(Bullshit!)

——马县长:"刘邦是个小人。"(Robin Hood is a common thief.)

——前汤师爷:"力拔山兮气盖世。"(With Samson's might and Solomon's wisdom!)

——马夫人"屁!"(Bullshit!)

这一段前汤师爷将马县长比作中国古人刘邦和项羽,西方观众并不能理解。翻译时运用归化技巧,转为西方观众能够理解的人物,如绿林好汉"罗宾汉",力大无穷的"参孙"(Samson),和以智慧闻名的"所罗门"(Solomon),更能引起他们的共鸣。

又如,影片《卧虎藏龙》中"八旗军布防严密,各有辖区",其中"八旗"就是一个有浓厚中国文化色彩的名词,如果将其直译为"baqi",则会令外国观众困惑不解,可以将其译为"the Royal Guard",让观众通过自己的文化背景理解源语言字幕的思想内容。

有时候,适当使用译入语中的习惯用语,更能传达出原字幕的幽默和风趣。如在《冰川世纪3》中,希德是一个十分搞笑的角色。他恳求曼尼把刚出生的小长毛象交给他抚养,并表示可以"work cheap"。

—Sid:Can I baby-sit for you? (我能给你家当保姆吗?)

—Manny:Not a chance. (想都别想。)

—Sid:Oh come on, I work cheap. (别这样嘛,我可以低薪上岗。)

"work cheap"译为中国观众熟悉的用语"低薪上岗",既惟妙惟肖地传达出希德的热心和急切,又能戳中中国观众的"笑点",取得很好的艺术效果。

为了充分传达电影的文化特色和语言魅力,有时也需要运用异化译法。如电影《功夫》对白中出现了"洪家铁线拳""昆仑派的蛤蟆功"等名词,由于各路"功夫"是该电影的重要内容,影片也以生动的电影画面表现了火云邪神使出"蛤蟆功"时的神态。因此,翻译时采用异化译法,尽量保留原文语言形式和文化特点。其中"洪家铁线拳"译为"Iron Fist from the Hung School","昆仑派的蛤蟆功"则译为"the Toad Style of Kwan Lun School"。

总之,在电影字幕翻译中,应将异化与归化两种译法有机结合起来,努力使电影字幕传达出源语言文化的特质,同时也应兼顾到读者的现实接受能力与译文的可读性,实现两者的动态平衡,使影片字幕翻译得准确而传神。

2. 浓缩和变通

突破字幕的时空局限性是字幕翻译的一个很大的挑战,因此,字幕翻译经常用到省略和浓缩的技巧。这并不是对原文的不忠实,相反,这正是基于电影字幕翻译特点而采用的翻译策略,目的是与原文在思想内容、风格等方面一致。省略和浓缩并非只是简单地将长句改成短句或者任意删减,而是要在保留原文关键信息的原则上,对原文信息进行精简和浓缩,最大限度地保留原文的信息和神韵。

如《让子弹飞》中,小六子邀请县长夫人跟他们回山上做压寨夫人,张麻子说:"人往高处走,水往低处流。"这是一句中国的俗语,其中的两个分句表达的是差不多的意思,翻译时可浓缩为一句:"One should always aim high."同样表达了原文的含义:人应该往高处走,县长夫人怎么可能跟着他们这帮土匪呢?

为电影配音所做的翻译,要求就更为复杂一些。除了考虑视觉因素,还要考虑与影片中的动作同步、口型一致。

如《武状元苏乞儿》的海外版中,苏灿与僧格林沁打斗时,苏灿以"虎鹤双形"迎战僧格林沁的"螳螂拳",并调侃说:

——苏灿:螳螂怎么能打得过老虎?况且还有一只鹤。

—A mantis can beat a tiger? Plus, I've got a hawk.

"鹤"的英文是crane,但是译者将其译为hawk(鹰)。这样变通的原因是,crane跟"鹤"发音口型不一致,而hawk发音则接近影片中苏灿说"鹤"的口型,这样,当观众看着电影,听着英文配音时,感到声音和画面协调一致,能够尽情欣赏影片而不受语言差异的干扰。

总之,在进行字幕翻译时,不仅要忠实于源语内容,还应充分关照译入语观众的审美意识和接受程度,巧妙地突破电影翻译的各种限制因素,达到良好的翻译效果。

【译作欣赏】

(1) What good the wings bear, if you couldn't feel the wind on your face?
如果不能感受到清风拂面,要翅膀何用? ——《天使之城》

(2) I would rather you remember me the way I was.
我宁愿你记住我原来的样子。 ——《剪刀手爱德华》

(3) A strong man can save himself; a great man can save another.

强者自救,圣者度人。——《肖申克的救赎》

(4) Your mind is like this water, my friend. When it is agitated, it becomes difficult to see, but if you allow it to settle, the answer becomes clear.

心若此水,乱则不明;若心静如潭,解决之道必将自现。——《功夫熊猫》

第三节 声名远播：广告翻译

一、广告语的基本特点

从语言和文体角度，广告语大致分为两大类：口语体和书面体。经典广告语的共同特点是引人入胜、说服力强。广告语的语言特征是：语法简单，句子短小，甚至单词、短语、从句等独立成句；选词上注意构思精巧，匠心独运，佳句、妙句、新词层出不穷；广泛运用修辞手段，如语意双关、文字游戏等，使人感到幽默中见智慧，创意里出新奇。句式上也极具鲜明特色，或行文工整、押韵对仗，或朗朗上口、音韵铿锵，或一鸣惊人、过目难忘，达到良好的宣传效果。总的来说，可以归纳为以下四个方面：吸引力（attractive—catch the reader's attention）、创造力（creative—project an image）、说服力（persuasive—urge the reader to act）和影响力（impressive—produce an impact）。

在翻译广告文字时，无论是英译汉还是汉译英，绝不能满足于字面上的翻译，必须充分运用翻译技巧，不仅追求准确、地道，还要把原文中的个性和言外之意传达出来。这样才能使译文尽量做到达意、传神和表形，收到意似、神似和形似的效果。

二、广告翻译的原则

广告翻译的最高原则不是传统的忠实而是创造性翻译。因为广告创作的灵魂是创意，广告翻译就是一种跨文化的信息再创作。成功的翻译能在译入语中再创作出通俗易懂、易读易记，又能有力促销产品的广告作品。创造性翻译比忠实、通顺、优雅的译文更为重要。

三、广告翻译的策略

1. 直译与异化翻译

直译（literal translation）是"把原来语言的语法结构转换为译文语言中最近似的对应结构"。异化翻译（foreignization translation），相对于归化翻译方法，较多地保留了外文的句式结构和表达方式，较少考虑目标受众的阅读习惯和理解方式。例如：

(1) Challenge the limits.

挑战极限。（Samsung）

(2) Above and beyond.

超越自我。(Land Rover)

(3) Life is wonderful.

活得精彩。(Ford)

(4) Pioneering the world.

敢为天下先。(Cadillac)

(5) He who loves me follows me.

爱我就跟随我。(Kappa)

以上广告词的英文原文都非常通俗易懂，表层意思和深层意思基本一致，译文采用了直译或语义翻译或异化翻译策略，语义和结构都忠实于原文，虽然读起来可能不像用母语原创的文本那样流畅，但明确传达出了表层和深层信息。

2. 意译或动态对等、功能对等翻译

"意译"(free translation)通常指取原文内容而舍弃其形式，容许译者有一定的创造性，但原文的基本信息应该保存。"动态对等"或"功能对等"(dynamic, or functional equivalence)，是指从语言意义到文体在译入语中用最切近而又最自然的对等语再现原语的信息，重点放在译文接受者的反应上。其共同点是翻译手法较为自由、灵活，翻译过程中通常考虑到了译文目标读者因文化而产生的阅读和理解上的差异，译文从读者角度看比较地道，可读性较强。例如：

(1) Ask for more!

渴望无限。(Pepsi Cola——百事可乐)

(2) Future for my future.

未来，为我而来。(雪佛兰)

(3) Every time a good time.

秒秒钟钟，欢聚欢笑。(MacDonald's——麦当劳)

(4) We care to provide service above and beyond the call of duty.

殷勤有加，风雨不改。(UPS——快递)

(5) Begin your own tradition.

代代相传由你开始。(Patek PhiliPPe Geneve Watch——百达翡丽)

虽然以上每一条译文的句子结构和关键词词义与原文都无法一一对应，但原广告词的精髓或深层意义仍然在译文中得以保留，译文的可读性等同于甚至超越原文。

3. 再创型翻译

再创型翻译(creative translation)策略，已经基本脱离原文范畴，译文与原文在表层意思上很少有相似之处，带有一定创造性，但又不是原创，而是重新创造。例如：

(1) Connecting people.

科技以人为本。(Nokia)

(2) Good to the last drop.

滴滴香浓,意犹未尽。(麦斯威尔咖啡)

(3) A great way to fly.

新加坡航空,飞越万里,超越一切。(Singapore Airlines——新加坡航空)

(4) It happens at the Hilton.

希尔顿酒店,有求必应。(Hilton)

(5) It's all within your reach.

联络世界,触及未来。(AT&T——电讯)

以上译文已基本脱离原文框架,属于重新创造。其中文文本从修辞学上讲都已经达到很高的水准,句子的精辟程度和可读性都不比原文差。而译文的意境往往比原文更深远。

4. 超额翻译

超额翻译(over-translation)指将原文某些关键词的词义进行挖掘、引申或扩充,将原文的深层意思加以发挥,使之突现。例如:

(1) Elegance is an attitude.

优雅态度,真我个性。(Longines——浪琴表)

(2) Beyond your imagination.

意想不到的天空。(Korean Air——大韩航空)

(3) Be good to yourself. Fly emirates.

纵爱自己,纵横万里。(Emirate——阿联酋航空)

(4) Any shape and size to Europe.

不同大小各种形状,火速直飞欧洲。(Federal Express——联邦快递)

上述广告译文显然语义上没有完全忠实于原文,部分信息原文中并不存在,但是因为增补,意境更加深远、内容更加贴切,效果更出色。

汉语里的四字成语,言简意赅,寓意深长,含义丰富。英语广告汉译时可充分利用译入语的文化和语言优势,使用大量的结构工整、押韵对仗而又通俗易懂的成语典故,不仅朗朗上口,而且便于记忆,在语义译出的基础上达到锦上添花的效果。例如:

(1) Trust us for life.

财务稳健,信守一生。(American International Assurance)

(2) Your future is our future.

与您并肩,迈向明天。(HSBC——汇丰银行)

(3) Taking the lead in a Digital World.

领先数码,超越永恒。(Samsung)

(4) Any time.

随时随地,准时无误。(TNT——快递服务)

(5) Focus on Life.

a. 人生难忘片段,永留印记。

b. 瞄准生活。(Olympus——相机)

5. 欠额翻译

如果广告原文写得不够精练,信息过剩,偶尔不妨采用欠额翻译(under-translation)策略。例如:

Overseas. Time set free overseas.

自由真义。(Vacheron Constantin——江诗丹顿)

总之,再创型翻译、超额翻译和欠额翻译虽然在理论上有悖于传统的"信、达、雅"的翻译标准,但广告翻译可以看成是"另类"翻译(specialized translation)。广告的目的是为了宣传和推销产品,为了达到理想的广告效应,试之无妨。

6. 不译

有时,英文广告中含一些短小精悍、表现力强的口号。当无法译出与原文同样惟妙惟肖的对应句时,可保留部分广告词不译。这种看似不伦不类的广告文体,却带着点异国情调,反而是一种时尚。正如年轻人日常交流中常夹杂英语单词一样,或许更能被受众接受,产生出奇制胜的效果。例如:

NEC Multimedia welcomes you home. (Slogan:)Just imagine.

这里变成你家!(口号:)Just imagine.(NEC Multimedia)

Open your eyes to the world. (Slogan:)The world's news leader.

CNN国际新闻网让您放眼看世界(口号:)The world's news leader. (CNN International)

两则广告中Just imagine和The world's news leader虽然保持不译,但随着华人英文水平的提高,理解不成问题。

课堂练习

1. 广告语有什么特点?英汉广告词有何差别?翻译广告需要什么策略?
2. 比较下列英汉广告词,说说你最喜欢哪个译文?为什么?

(1) Good to the last drop.

滴滴香浓,意犹未尽。(麦斯威尔咖啡)

(2) Obey your thirst.

服从你的渴望。(雪碧)

(3) Just do it.

只管去做。(耐克运动鞋)

(4) Keep moving.

永不止步。(安踏)

(5) The taste is great.

味道好极了。(雀巢咖啡)

(6) Feel the new space.

感受新境界。(三星电子)

(7) Intelligence everywhere.

智慧演绎,无处不在。(摩托罗拉手机)

(8) The choice of a new generation.

新一代的选择。(百事可乐)

(9) Start ahead.

成功之路,从头开始。(飘柔)

(10) A diamond lasts forever.

钻石恒久远,一颗永流传。(戴比尔斯)

翻译视听

香奈儿 N°5 香水最新广告词

(1) 看视频填单词。

It's not a journey; every _____ ends but we go on. The world _____ and we turn with it. Plans _____, dreams take over. But _____ I go, there you are:my _____, my fate, my forture.

(2) 请将广告译成汉语。

(3) 比较英汉版本的语言特色,分析一下译文运用了哪些翻译策略。

译作欣赏

对比分析下列广告语的语言和文化特色。

(1) Time is what you make of it.

天长地久。(斯沃奇手表)

(2) Make yourself heard.

理解就是沟通。(爱立信)

(3) No business too small, no problem too big.

没有不做的小生意,没有解决不了的大问题。(IBM 公司)

(4) Let's make things better.

让我们做得更好。(飞利浦电子)

(5) The relentless pursuit of perfection.

追求完美,永无止境。(雷克萨斯)

(6) Feel the new space.

感受新境界。(三星电子)

(7) Engineered to move the human spirit.

人类精神的动力。(梅塞德斯-奔驰)

(8) Communication unlimited.

沟通无极限。(摩托罗拉)

(9) Impossible made possible.

使不可能变为可能。(佳能打印机)

(10) Can't beat the real thing.

挡不住的诱惑。(可口可乐)

(11) Anything is possible.

一切皆有可能。(李宁体育用品)

(12) Take Toshiba, take the world.

拥有东芝,拥有世界。(东芝电子)

(13) Ideas for life.

为生活着想。(松下电子)

(14) M&Ms melt in your mouth, not in your hand.

只溶在口,不溶在手。(M&Ms巧克力)

(15) The imitable jeans and the inimitable coolness.

不同的酷,相同的裤。(李维斯牛仔)

第四节 正确引领：标识语翻译

随着在我国境内的国际交流日益频繁，国内各公共场所的标识语越来越倾向于使用中英双语，以方便来自不同国家的来访者。但随之也出现了一些不够准确和规范的标识语翻译，误导受众，造成不良后果。本章中介绍一些常用的标识语的翻译方法。

一、标识语的类型

标识语可分成三大类型，即指示性标识语、管理性标识语和广告性标识语。
(1) 设置指示性标识语的目的是向公众显示各类功能信息。例如：
投诉电话　Complaints Hotlines
自动扶梯　Escalators
装卸区域　Loading Zone
(2) 管理性标识语给受众发出某种警示、限制信号以及强制性命令。例如：
注意防滑　Caution! Wet Floor!
当心脚下　Watch Your Step
(3) 广告性标识语包括服务承诺、商业推销和公益性广告。例如：
八折优惠　20% Off
宾至如归　A Home Away from Home
买一赠一　Buy One and Get One Free

二、英语标识语的特点

英语标识语具有短小精悍、言简意赅、规范标准等特点。首先，受展示空间限制，标识语要尽量简洁，避免冗长；同时，为警示公众，标识语要清楚醒目、突显重点。因此常常大量使用静态词汇、缩略语，管理性标识语中还常常使用祈使语气。另外，为了有效交流、避免误会，标识语往往有约定俗成的表达方式。

三、英语标识语的翻译原则

1. 力求简洁、精确

公共场所的标识语，必须准确无误地给大众传递相关信息。由于流动人群是其受众，标识语必须突显、醒目、简单、易懂。因此，标识语常常只使用实词、关键词、核心词，而往往省略冠词、代词和助动词。例如：
免票入场　Admission Free（名词和形容词）

酒水另付　Beverage Not Included（名词、副词和过去分词）

送客止步　Passengers Only（名词和副词）

如果只使用名词仍能保证表达内容完整，翻译时应尽量使用名词，而省略其他句子成分。例如：

此处有炸药，注意安全　Danger：Explosive

2. 使用规范标准语汇

很多与日常生活相关的英语标识语都是各个国家通用的，为避免模糊、歧义和误解导致的不良后果，翻译时应做好功课，查找通用的规范和标准的表达，或是约定俗成的语汇，例如：

Baggage Depository　存包处

Duty Free Shop　免税店

Foreign Exchange　外币兑换

3. 采用一致的缩略语

为了使用方便，大众最熟悉、常接触、使用频率较高的公共服务设施，常常会使用缩略语来进行标示。翻译时要注意使用国际通用的缩略语。例如：

TI(Tourism Information)　旅游咨询

F&B(Food & Beverage)　餐饮服务

4. 使用现在时态

对于特定区域内的公众来讲，标识语常常给予此时此地行为的指示、提示、限制或强制。时态常常限于现在时。例如：

当心，此门朝外开　Caution：Door Opens Outwards

四、管理性标识语的翻译技巧

需要翻译成英语的，多半是管理性标识语。这里重点谈谈管理性标识语的翻译技巧。具体说来，管理性标识语有以下三类。

1. 警示性标识语

警示性标识语用于提示或者警告受众需要注意的事项，常使用祈使句。或者使用 watch(for), caution, mind, beware of 等表达，提醒大家注意某事，也可以直接使用 danger, warning, attention 等词语发出某种警告。例如：

当心脚下　Watch Your Step

注意防滑　Caution! Wet Floor!

小心碰头　Mind Your Head

有狗，请勿靠近　Beware of Dogs

小心落物　Danger! Falling Objects!

2. 限制性标识语

限制性标识语表示专用或对某些人或车辆行为等的限制，可用...unless, ...

only, no...excepted..., no...except (for)...,或其他表示限制的词语来翻译。例如：

  轮椅专用　Wheelchairs Only

  禁止站人，卡车装卸时例外　No Standing Except Trucks Loading & Unloading

  靠右行驶，超车例外　Keep Right unless Overtaking

3. 强制性标识语

  强制性标识语具有一定的权威，表示禁令，对违反者要按规定处以惩罚。这类标识语语气强硬，不容商量。常用 no, do not, must, be strictly prohibited, not allowed/permitted, keep off/away 等；penalties apply, fine, prosecuted（提示公诉、罚款、责任自负、法办）等句型则表示惩罚。例如：

  严禁乱涂乱画　No Graffiti

  乘船时请勿与驾驶员交谈，以免影响驾驶　Do Not Talk to the Pilot When Boat Is On

  儿童必须成人陪同　Children Must Be Accompanied by Adults

  核心景区，严禁烟火　Smoking and Open Flames Are Strictly Prohibited

【课堂练习】

以下哪个标识语表达较规范：

1. 闲人免进
    a. Staff Only
    b. Strangers Are Forbidden
2. 自行车请推行
    a. Please Walk Your Cycle
    b. Please Push Your Bicycle
3. 紧急逃生窗口
    a. Emergency Flee Window
    b. Emergency Exit Window
4. 谨防被盗！
    a. Attention! Pickpockets!
    b. Protect Stolen!
5. 请勿带狗入内
    a. Please Don't Come in with Dogs
    b. No Dogs Allowed
6. 当心脚下

a. Be Careful of Your Feet

   b. Watch Your Step

7. 保护文物,爱护栏杆

   a. Keep Off the Railings

   b. Help Protect the Cultural Relics，Help Protect the Railings

8. 请勿拍照

   a. No Taking Photo

   b. No Photography

拓展阅读

1. 校园常见标识语

（1）保护环境,禁丢弃物　No Littering

（2）请勿占座　No Seat-Saving　/　Please Don't Save Seats

（3）请看管好贵重物品　Please Don't Lose Sight of Your Valuables

（4）小草青青,踏之何忍　Keep Off the Grass

（5）请勿乱涂乱画　No Graffiti

（6）前方学校　School Ahead

（7）献血拯救生命　Donate Blood to Save Lives

（8）你已进入电子监控区域　These Premises Are Protected by Closed Circuit Television with Video Recording

2. 旅游观光购物常见标识语

（1）摩天轮　Ferris Wheel

（2）过山车　Roller Coaster

（3）注意保管好个人用品　Please Do Not Leave Your Belongings Unattended

（4）油漆未干　Wet Paint!

（5）试衣间　Fitting Room

（6）更衣室　Locker Room

（7）禁止食用非本店食品　No Outside Food

（8）洗手间　Toilet(英国/澳大利亚)　Restroom(美国)
　　 Washroom(加拿大)　Lavatory(飞机上)

第五节　品味中国：中国菜谱翻译

一、中国菜谱翻译的原则

菜谱是一种实用性极强的文本，翻译应强调其功能性，即准确、忠实传递菜肴的信息，包括其配料和烹饪方法，供食客了解和选择。同时要尊重食客的审美需求，让人一看就大倒胃口的翻译是一定要避免的。如将"红烧狮子头"翻译为"burnt lion's head"，不仅信息传递不清，还让人食欲全无。

二、中国菜谱翻译的技巧

前面说过，菜谱翻译的目的是将信息准确传递给阅读者，中国菜谱译为英文时，可参照西方菜谱的表达方式。完整的菜名翻译公式是：烹饪方法＋形状/口感＋主料＋配料。但为了简洁，一般菜肴翻译不用包含以上所有信息，只需要译出最重要的信息。具体来说，有以下几种翻译技巧。

1. 重点介绍主料的翻译方法

主料＋ with/in ＋ 配料/汤/酱。例如：

酸汤鱼　Fish in Sour Soup

炸酱面　Noodles with Soy Bean Paste

北川凉粉　Clear Noodles in Chili Sauce

2. 重点介绍烹制方法的翻译方法

1) 介绍菜肴的料理方法和主料

做法(过去分词)＋主料(名称/形状)。例如：

油焖春笋　Braised Bamboo Shoot

2) 介绍菜肴的料理方法、主料和配料

做法(过去分词)＋主料(名称/形状)＋ 配料。例如：

大煮干丝　Raised Shredded Chicken with Ham and Dried Tofu

3) 介绍菜肴的料理方法、主料和汤汁

做法(过去分词)＋主料(名称/形状)＋ with/in ＋汤汁。例如：

京酱肉丝　Sautéed Shredded Pork in Sweet Bean Sauce

开水白菜　Steamed Chinese Cabbage in Supreme Soup

3. 重点介绍口感的翻译方法

清明团子　Sweet Green Rice Ball

脆皮乳猪　Crispy BBQ Suckling Pig

4. 介绍创始人或发源地

菜名中含创始人或地名的,可以保留人名和地名。

(1) 菜肴的创始人(发源地)+主料。例如:

东坡肉　Dongpo Pork

麻婆豆腐　Mapo Tofu

(2) 做法(动词过去式)+主辅料+人名/地名+Style。例如:

北京炒肝　Stewed Liver, Beijing Style

北京炸酱面　Noodles with Soy Bean Paste, Beijing Style

5. 直接以汉语拼音翻译菜名

(1) 具有中国特色的,且其拼音已被外国人接受的传统食品,本着约定俗成和推广中国文化的原则,使用汉语拼音。例如:

饺子　Jiaozi　　　　　豆腐　Tofu

杂碎　Chop Suey　　　馄饨　Wonton

烧麦　Shaomai

(2) 正式的菜单中,可在汉语拼音后标注英文注释,让阅读者了解配料、做法和名称由来。例如:

驴打滚　Lǘdagunr(Glutinous Rice Rolls with Sweet Bean Flour)

佛跳墙　Fotiaoqiang—Steamed Abalone with Shark's Fin and Fish Maw in Broth (Lured by its delicious aroma, even the Buddha jumped over the wall to eat this dish.)

锅贴　Guotie (Pan-Fried Meat Dumplings)

窝头　Wotou(Steamed Black Rice or Corn Bun)

课堂练习

请将以下菜肴的中英文名称配对:

(1) 生煎包　　　　　　　　a. Stewed Chick with Mushroom

(2) 开水白菜　　　　　　　b. Braised Sea Cucumbers with Spring Onions

(3) 烧鹅　　　　　　　　　c. Stir-Fried Shrimps

(4) 油爆虾　　　　　　　　d. Sautéed Beef with Pickled Bamboo Shoots

(5) 小鸡炖蘑菇　　　　　　e. Steamed Chinese Cabbage in Supreme Soup

(6) 葱烧海参　　　　　　　f. Pan-Fried Bun Stuffed with Pork

(7) 酸笋炒牛肉　　　　　　g. Roast Goose

拓展阅读

1. 下面是《舌尖上的中国》中部分地方小吃的翻译,找到你家乡的美味了吗?

莲藕排骨汤　Lotus Root and Rib Soup
炸藕夹　Deep-Fried Lotus Root Sandwich
油焖春笋　Braised Bamboo Shoot
酸菜鱼　Boiled Fish with Pickled Cabbage and Chili
酸辣藕丁　Hot and Sour Lotus Root
馒头　Steamed Bread
葱油椒盐花卷　Steamed Twisted Rolls with Scallion and Spicy Salt
腊汁肉夹馍　Chinese Hamburger
羊肉泡馍　Pita Bread Soaked in Lamb Soup
兰州拉面　Lanzhou Hand-Pulled Noodles
青菜炒年糕　Rice Cake Stir-Fried with Vegetables
毛蟹炒年糕　Rice Cake Stir-Fried with Crabs
扁豆焖面　Braised Noodles with Lentil
山西焖面　Shanxi Braised Noodles
清明团子　Sweet Green Rice Ball
鲜虾云吞面　Wonton Noodle with Shrimps
大煮干丝　Raised Shredded Chicken with Ham and Dried Tofu
豆腐脑　Tofu Curd
香炸奶豆腐　Fried Dried Milk Cake
蒙古奶茶　Mongolia Milky Tea
炸乳扇　Fried Dairy Fan
烤羊排　Baked Lamp Chop
红烧毛豆腐　Stinky Tofu Braised in Soy Sauce
绍兴醉鸡　Shaoxing Chicken in Wine
酸菜白肉　Pickled Chinese Cabbage with Plain Boiled Pork
酸菜饺子　Dumpling of Pickled Chinese Cabbage

2. 北京奥运会菜单中英文对照

1) 凉菜

八宝辣酱　Eight Delicacies in Hot Sauce
夫妻肺片　Pork Lungs in Chili Sauce
川北凉粉　Clear Noodles in Chili Sauce
棒棒鸡　Bon Bon Chicken
麻辣小龙虾　Hot and Spicy Crayfish
扒猪脸　Snout
桂花糯米藕　Steamed Lotus Root Stuffed with Sweet Sticky Rice
醉蟹　Liquor-Soaked Crabs

2) 酒水

茅台　Moutai

红星二锅头　Red Star Erguotou

衡水老白干　Hengshui Laobaigan

青岛啤酒　Tsing Tao Beer

长城干红　Great Wall Red Wine

绍兴女儿红　Nu'er Hong

3) 茶

碧螺春　Biluochun Tea

大红袍　Dahongpao Tea

陈年普洱　Aged Pu'er Tea

祁门红茶　Keemun Black Tea

茉莉花茶　Jasmine Tea

4) 汤

西红柿蛋花汤　Tomato and Egg Soup

紫菜蛋花汤　Seaweed and Egg Soup

鱼头豆腐汤　Fish Head and Tofu Soup

老鸭汤　Duck Soup

酸菜粉丝汤　Pickled Cabbage and Vermicelli Soup

萝卜丝鲫鱼汤　Crucian Carp Soup with Shredded Turnips

黄豆排骨汤　Pork Ribs and Soy Bean Soup

木瓜花生炖鸡脚　Chicken Paw Soup with Papaya and Peanut

5) 主菜

(1) 川菜：

麻婆豆腐　Mapo Tofu

回锅肉　Sautéed Sliced Pork with Pepper and Chili

干烧鱼翅　Dry-Braised Shark's Fin

豆花肉蟹　Sautéed Hardshell Crab with Tofu Pudding

坛子鸡　Chicken in Pot

樟茶鸭　Smoked Duck, Sichuan Style

魔芋鸭　Braised Duck with Shredded Konjak

(2) 粤菜：

佛跳墙　Fotiaoqiang

叉烧　BBQ Pork

烧鹅　Roast Goose

白斩鸡　Chopped Boiled Chicken

脆皮乳猪　Crispy BBQ Suckling Pig
脆皮乳鸽　Crispy Pigeon

(3) 鲁菜：

葱烧海参　Braised Sea Cucumbers with Spring Onions
九转大肠　Braised Intestines in Brown Sauce

(4) 北京菜：

北京烤鸭　Peking Duck
京酱肉丝　Sautéed Shredded Pork in Sweet Bean Sauce
羊蝎子　Lamb Spine Hot Pot

(5) 贵州菜：

酸汤鱼　Fish in Sour Soup
花江狗肉　Huajiang Dog Meat

(6) 湘菜：

剁椒鱼头　Steamed Fish Head with Diced Hot Red Peppers
莲蓬扣肉　Braised Pork with Lotus Seeds
农家小炒肉　Shredded Pork with Vegetables
干锅茶树菇　Griddle Cooked Tea Tree Mushrooms

(7) 淮扬菜：

红烧狮子头　Stewed Pork Ball in Brown Sauce
蜜汁火方　Braised Ham in Honey Sauce

(8) 浙江菜：

西湖醋鱼　West Lake Fish in Vinegar Gravy
东坡肉　Braised Dongpo Pork

(9) 东北菜：

小鸡炖蘑菇　Stewed Chick with Mushroom
酱骨架　Braised Spare Ribs in Brown Sauce

(10) 新疆菜：

大盘鸡　Braised Chicken with Potato and Green Pepper
孜然寸骨　Sautéed Spare Ribs with Cumin

(11) 广西菜：

啤酒鸭　Stewed Duck in Beer
酸笋炒牛肉　Sautéed Beef with Pickled Bamboo Shoots

(12) 上海菜：

油爆虾　Stir-Fried Shrimps
毛蟹炒年糕　Sautéed Hardshell Crab with Rice Cake

(13) 江西菜：

三杯鸡　Stewed Chicken with Three Cups Sauce

藜蒿炒腊肉　Sautéed Preserved Pork with Artemisia Selengensis

(14) 云南菜：

汽锅鸡　Steam Pot Chicken

6) 蔬菜

开水白菜　Steamed Chinese Cabbage in Supreme Soup

清炒红菜薹　Sautéed Chinese Kale

米汤豆苗　Sautéed Pea Sprouts in Rice Soup

干煸四季豆　Dry-Fried French Beans with Minced Pork and Preserved Vegetables

7) 主食

(1) 粥：

艇仔粥　Tingzai Porridge

红豆粥　Red Bean Porridge

(2) 粉：

干炒牛河　Stir-Fried Rice Noodles with Beef

过桥米线　Yunnan Rice Noodles

桂林米粉　Guilin Rice Noodles

(3) 面：

热干面　Hot Noodles with Sesame Paste

炸酱面　Noodles with Soy Bean Paste

担担面　Noodles, Sichuan Style

两面黄　Pan-Fried Noodles

刀削面　Sliced Noodles

臊子面　Noodle with Pork

羊肉泡馍　Pita Bread Soaked in Lamb Soup

狗不理包子　Go Believe

叉烧包　Steamed BBQ Pork Bun

生煎包　Pan-Fried Bun Stuffed with Pork

红油抄手　Meat Dumplings in Spicy Sauce

(4) 饭：

八宝饭　Eight Delicacies Rice

鱼翅捞饭　Fin Rice

手抓饭　Xinjiang Rice

扬州炒饭　Yangzhou Fried Rice

海南鸡饭　Hainanese Chicken Rice

8）饭后甜点

（1）甜品：

杨枝甘露　Chilled Mango Sago Cream with Pomelo

双皮奶　Stewed Milk Beancurd

龟苓膏　Guiling Jelly

蛋挞　Egg Tart

驴打滚　Ludagunr

醪糟汤圆　Tangyuan in Fermented Glutinous Rice Soup

冰糖葫芦　Bingtanghulu

（2）小吃：

豆汁　Douzhir

爆肚儿　Soiled Pork Tripe

天津十八街麻花　Tianjin Hemp Flowers

油炸臭豆腐　Deep-Fried Fermented Tofu

（3）水果：

香梨　Xinjiang Pear

哈密瓜　Hami Melon

玫瑰香葡萄　Muscat Hamburg

广东荔枝　Litchi

烟台苹果　Yantai Apple

赣南脐橙　Jiangxi Navel Orange

第四章

中国文化翻译精选

中国文化博大精深、绚丽多彩。传播中国文化是当代大学生的责任和义务。大学英语四、六级考试也把对中国文化的翻译和介绍纳入考试范畴。然而在教学中我们发现学生在翻译这类文章时存在很多困难,最明显的是缺乏相关词汇和表达的积累。在此,我们精选了部分汉译英翻译示例及相关词汇。

第一节 文明传承:传统文化

1. 历史与文明

【例文 1】

丝 绸 之 路

闻名于世的丝绸之路是一系列连接东西方的路线。丝绸之路延伸6000多公里。得名于古代中国的丝绸贸易。丝绸之路上的贸易在中国、南亚、欧洲和中东文明发展中发挥了重要作用。正是通过丝绸之路,中国的造纸、火药、指南针、印刷等四大发明才被引介到世界各地。同样,中国的丝绸、茶叶和瓷器(porcelain)也传遍全球。物质文化的交流是双向的。欧洲也通过丝绸之路出口各种商品和植物,满足中国市场的需要。(2013年12月CET-6真题)

【参考译文】

The world-famous Silk Road is a series of routes connecting the West and East. Extending more than 6000 kilometers, the Silk Road gets its name from the ancient Chinese silk trade. Trade on the Silk Road played a significant role in the development of the civilization of China, South Asia, Europe and the Middle East. It was through the Silk Road that the four great ancient Chinese inventions of paper making, gunpowder, the compass and the printing were introduced to the world. Likewise, Chinese silk, tea and porcelain were also spread throughout the globe. The exchange of material culture went both ways, with Europe also exporting a wide range of goods and plants via the Silk Road to meet the demands of the Chinese market.

【例文 2】

中国人的姓名

在当代中国,汉族人的姓名很少超过三个字——第一是姓,第二、三字为名,名被赋予意义。这与古人的姓名构成不同。古人的姓名通常包含四个部分——依次为姓、名、字和号。字为大家所熟知。在古代,人们不但可以通过名或字,而且可以通过号来辨别身份。尽管古人无法选择姓和名,但可以自己取号。根据当时的习俗,只有成年才取号。人们以此方式告诉他人,人生已进入新阶段。自己已经成年,可以追逐自己的梦想了。大家相互称字以示尊重。

【参考译文】

A modern Han Chinese name rarely has more than three characters—with the first character being the surname, and the second and third a connotative(内涵的) given name. This is very different from the way ancient Chinese names were formed. An ancient Chinese name often included four components:first the family name, followed by the given name, then what's known as the "style"(字) and the alias(号). In ancient China, one could be identified not only by the given name or the style after the surname, but also by the alias. Although one had no choice of surname or given name, one could choose his own alias. According to the custom of the time, people chose their alias when they entered adulthood. This was a way of telling others that their course in life had changed and that they were now adults and moving toward their goals. People called one another by the style to show mutual respect.

(编译自李萍. 中国文化背景[M]. 北京:世界图书出版公司,1998.)

【重点词汇】

四大发明(造纸术、火药、指南针、印刷)　the Four Great Ancient Chinese Inventions (papermaking, gunpowder, compass and printing)

文房四宝(笔、墨、纸、砚)　the Four Treasure of the Study(brush, ink, paper, and ink stone)

儒家文化	Confucianism	孟子	Mencius
《诗经》	*The Classic of Poetry*	中医	Traditional Chinese Medicine
针灸	acupuncture	京剧	Beijing Opera
太极拳	Tai Chi	相声	cross-talk/comic dialogue
农历	lunar calendar	印/玺	seal
朝代	dynasty	战国	the Warring States period
鸦片战争	the Opium War	五四运动	the May 4th Movement

抗日战争　the War of Resistance Against Japan
"文化大革命"　the Cultural Revolution

2. 民间艺术与传统食物

【例文 1】

中　国　结

中国结是典型的中国本土艺术。这是一门独特的传统中国民间手工编织艺术。每个绳结只使用一根线,根据形状和意义而命名。中国人使用绳结,不仅用来固定和包装,而且用来记录事件和纯粹装饰。"结"意味着团结、友谊、和平、温暖、婚姻和爱情等。中国结常用来表达良好的祝愿,包括幸福、繁荣、友爱和辟邪。中国结以其古典、优雅的图案,丰富的材料和日新月异的变化,既实用又具有装饰性,充分体现了中国文化的魅力,是中国人民的文化遗产。

【参考译文】

Chinese knots are typical local arts of China. Chinese knotting is a distinctive and traditional Chinese folk handicraft woven separately from one piece of thread and named according to its shape and meaning. Chinese people used knots not only for fastening and wrapping but also for recording events and pure decoration. "Knot" means reunion, friendship, peace, warmth, marriage and love, etc. Chinese knots are often employed to express good wishes including happiness, prosperity, love and the absence of evil. The Chinese knot, with its classic and graceful patterns, the multitude of materials as well as ever-changing variations, is both practical and ornamental, fully reflecting the grace of Chinese culture as the great cultural heritage of the Chinese people.

(编译自段义涛.中国文化英语80主题[M].北京:中国宇航出版社,2010.)

【例文 2】

岐山臊子面

岐山臊子的做法更为讲究。肉丁切得薄而匀,干焙至透明状,再配以醋和秦椒辣面,文火慢炒。上等的臊子应该是色泽鲜红纯正,口感酸辣突出。这样一勺色泽油亮、辣而不燥的红油臊子,正是岐山臊子面的精髓所在。

【参考译文】

The methods to make the ingredients for the Qishan saozi noodles are very particular. Meat is chopped into thin and even dices and dry-fried until they turn transparent. Add vinegar and chili and fry the meat on slow fire. The good-quality ingredients for Qishan saozi noodles are red in color, sour and spicy in the taste. The bright color and spicy taste are the essence of Qishan saozi noodles.

(节选自《舌尖上的中国》(英文版)。)

【重点词汇】

民间艺术	folk art	剪纸	paper cutting
书法	calligraphy	刺绣	embroidery
踩高跷	stilt walking	风筝	kite
泥塑	clay sculpture	皮影戏	shadow play
木偶戏	puppet show	中国结	Chinese knot
红白喜事	weddings and funerals	风水	Feng shui/Geomantic Omen

"传统食物"词汇见第三章第五节。

3. 风景名胜与传统建筑

【例文1】

长 城

长城是人类创造的世界奇迹之一。如果你到了中国却没去过长城,就像到了巴黎没有去看看埃菲尔铁塔,或者就像到了埃及没有去看金字塔一样。人们常说:"不到长城非好汉。"实际上,长城最初只是一些断断续续的城墙,直到秦朝统一中国后才将其连成长城。然而,今天我们看到的长城——东起山海关,西至嘉峪关——大部分是在明代修建的。

【参考译文】

The Great Wall is one of the wonders of the world created by human beings. If you come to China without climbing the Great Wall, it's just like going to Paris without visiting the Eiffel Tower; or going to Egypt without visiting the Pyramids. An old saying goes like this—"He who has never been to the Great Wall is not a true man." In fact, it began as independent walls for different states when it was first built, and did not become the "Great Wall" until the Qin Dynasty. However, the wall we see today, from Shanhaiguan Pass in the east to Jiayuguan Pass in the west, was mostly built during the Ming Dynasty.

(引自http://www.doc88.com/p-9982983029029.html)

【例文2】

胡 同

北京有无数的胡同(hutong)。平民百姓在胡同里的生活给古都北京带来了无穷的魅力。北京的胡同不仅仅是当地居民的生活环境,而且还是一门建筑艺术。通常,胡同内有一个四合院或大杂院,房间够4到10个家庭的差不多20口人住。所以,胡同里的生活充满了友善和人情味。如今,随着社会和经济的飞速发展,很多胡同被新的高楼大厦所取代。但愿胡同可以保留下来。

【参考译文】

In Beijing, there are numerous hutongs. The life of common people in hutongs brings endless charm to the ancient capital, Beijing. The hutong in Beijing is not only the living environment of local residents but also a kind of architecture. Usually, there is a Siheyuan, or a traditional quadrangle house with a courtyard in a hutong, with rooms shared by about 20 people of 4 to 10 families. Therefore, life in hutong is full of friendliness and genuine humanity. Nowadays, with rapid social and economic development, many hutongs are replaced by new buildings. I hope that hutongs can be preserved.

(引自 http://www.examw.com/cet4/trans/438384/)

【例文3】

西 安

西安是古丝绸之路的起点,也是中国历史上建都最多的城市之一。新发掘的秦兵马俑被称为"世界第八大奇迹";大雁塔、鼓楼是唐代留下来的建筑;您可以到杨贵妃沐浴的华清池去泡温泉澡;作为炎黄子孙还可以去拜谒离西安不远的黄帝陵。在西安还可以欣赏到仿唐音乐和歌舞,品尝唐菜。

Xi'an, the starting point of the ancient Silk Road, was capital intermittently for many dynasties in Chinese history. The life-size terracotta warriors and horses of the Qin Dynasty, unearthed recently, are prasied as the "eighth wonder of the world". Other interesting sites in the vicinity are Dayan Ta (Great Wild Goose Pagoda) and Gu Lou (Drum Tower), both erected in the Tang Dynasty; and the Huaqing Hot Spring where visitors may bathe in the warm mineral water. This site used to be the private baths for Yang Guifei, favorite concubine of a Tang emperor. If you are of Chinese descent, you may pay tribute to the tomb of Huangdi (Yellow Emperor), the first Chinese emperor. In addition, tourists will enjoy the pleasing Tang music and dance, as well as the duplication of fancy Tang dishes there.

(引自魏志成,余军. 汉英比较翻译教程练习[M]. 北京:清华大学出版社,2006.)

【重点词汇】

名川	great rivers	瀑布	waterfalls
名山	famous mountains	自然保护区	nature reserves
宫殿	palaces	园林	gardens
古镇	towns	古塔	towers
石窟	grottoes	蒙古包	Mongolian yurt

烽火台　beacon tower　　　　　　鼓楼　drum tower
华表　ornamental column　　　　乐山大佛　Leshan Giant Buddha
九寨沟　Jiuzhaigou Valley　　　　孔庙　Confucius Temple
秦始皇陵　the Mausoleum of Emperor Qinshihuang
兵马俑　terracotta warriors and horses

4. 传统节日

【例文 1】

春　节

中国新年是中国最重要的传统节日，在中国也被称为春节。新年的庆祝活动从除夕开始一直延续到元宵节，即从农历最后一个月的最后一天至新年第一个月的第十五天。各地欢度春节的习俗和传统有很大差异，但通常每个家庭都会在除夕夜团聚，一起吃年夜饭。为驱厄运、迎好运，家家户户都会进行大扫除。人们还会在门上粘贴红色的对联，对联的主题为健康、发财和好运。其他的活动还有放鞭炮、发红包和探亲访友等。

Chinese New Year is the most important traditional Chinese holiday. In China, it is also known as the Spring Festival. New Year celebrations run from Chinese New Year's Eve, the last day of the last month of the lunar calendar, to the Lantern Festival on the 15th day of the first month. Customs and traditions concerning the celebration of the Chinese New Year vary widely from place to place. However, New Year's Eve is usually an occasion for Chinese families to gather for the annual reunion dinner. It is also traditional for every family to thoroughly clean the house in order to sweep away ill fortune and to bring in good luck. And doors will be decorated with red couplets with themes of health, wealth and good luck. Other activities include lighting firecrackers, giving money in red envelopes, and visiting relatives and friends.

（引自 http://www.cet.edu.cn/slj.htm）

【例文 2】

清　明　节

每年 4 月 4 日到 6 日的清明节是传统的扫墓的日子。在这一天，人们祭悼去世的亲人，到先人的坟头上扫墓。唐朝著名诗人杜牧有一首著名的诗，描述了四月初令人伤感的一幕场景："清明时节雨纷纷，路上行人欲断魂。"与清明节扫墓的悲哀相反，人们在这个日子尽情欣赏自然美景。清明时节，树木和小草吐绿，大自然生机盎然。从古代起，人们就有春游的习俗。如今，清明节是中国内地的法定假日。

【参考译文】

The Qingming Festival, the traditional tomb-sweeping day, falls on April 4—

6 each year. It's an occasion to commemorate loved ones who have departed and pay respect to ancestors at their graves. A well-known poem by Du Mu in Tang Dynasty tells of a sad scene in early April: "A drizzling rain falls like tears on the Mourning Day; the mourner's heart is going to break on his way…" In contrast to the sadness of the tomb-sweeping, people feast their eyes on the beautiful nature on this day, which happens to be a vigorous spring time when the trees and grass begin to turn green. Since ancient times, people have followed the custom of spring outing. Today, the Qingming Festival is a national holiday in mainland China.

(参考 http://www.putclub.com/html/exam/cet6/2014/0418/85206.html)

【重点词汇】

(1) 春节　the Spring Festival：

除夕　Chinese New Year's Eve/Eve of the Spring Festival

春联　spring couplets

爆竹　fire cracker

年画　(traditional) New Year pictures

压岁钱　New Year gift-money

农历/阴历　Chinese lunar calendar

团圆饭　family reunion dinner

拜年　pay a new year visit

(2) 元宵节　the Lantern Festival：

花灯　festival lantern

灯谜　lantern riddles

舞龙/狮　dragon/lion dance

(3) 清明节　the Tomb Sweeping Day/the Qingming Festival：

扫墓　sweep tombs/pay respect to ancestors at their graves

祭祖　offer sacrifices to the forefathers/ancestors

纪念亡者　honor the deceased/mourn the dead

踏青　go out for an outing/enjoy the greenery of springtime

(4) 端午节　the Dragon Boat Festival：

赛龙舟　dragon boat race

亡灵　departed soul

忠臣　loyal minister

(5) 七夕节　the Double-Seventh Day/the Chinese Valentine's Day：

银河　the Milky Way

牛郎、织女　Cowherd, Weaver Maid

(6) 中秋节　the Mid-Autumn Festival：

赏月　admire/appreciate the full moon

月饼　moon cake

团圆　reunion

(7) 重阳节　the Chongyang Festival/the Double-Ninth Festival/the Seniors' Day：

尊老　respect the elderly

第二节 文化传播：现代社会

1. 社会发展

【例文1】

中 国 梦

几千年的中国文化充实着中国梦，同时，过去三十几年的改革开放也激励着中国梦。中国梦最显著的特征是包容性和双赢合作。这些也是使中国梦扩大到全球影响范围和被其他国家的人民认可的基本特征。中国梦是民族复兴的梦。它是建设一个强大繁荣的国家，给中国人民带来幸福生活的梦。中国梦需要维持稳定、健康的经济发展，科学管理社会，以及有效应对外部发展的风险和挑战。

【参考译文】

The Chinese dream has been enriched by thousands of years of Chinese culture and inspired by the past three decades of reform and opening-up. The most noticeable features of Chinese dream include inclusiveness and win-win cooperation. These are the very features that will enable the Chinese dream to expand its global reach and be recognized by people of other nations. The Chinese dream is the dream of national rejuvenation. It's the dream of building a powerful and prosperous state, the dream of bringing happiness to the lives of Chinese people. It entails sustaining steady and healthy economic growth, scientifically managing the Chinese society, and effectively responding to the risks and challenges of external development.

（引自 http://www.putclub.com/html/exam/cet6/2014/0418/85206.html）

【例文2】

中国航天事业

中国政府把发展航天事业作为国家整体发展战略的重要组成部分，始终坚持为了和平而探索和利用外层空间。近年来，中国航天事业发展迅速，在若干重要技术领域跻身世界先进行列。航天活动在中国经济建设和社会发展中发挥着越来越重要的作用。

The Chinese government makes the space industry an important part of the nation's overall development strategy, and adheres to exploration and utilization of outer space for peaceful purposes. Over the past few years, China's space industry has developed rapidly and China ranks among the world's leading countries in certain major areas of space technology. Space activities play an increasingly important role in China's economic and social development.

（引自魏志成，余军. 汉英比较翻译教程练习［M］. 北京：清华大学出版社，2006.）

【例文3】

老龄化社会

如今，中国正步入老龄化社会，因此独生子女一代面临着巨大的工作和生活压力。中国政府开始适当调整计划生育政策，允许一些家庭在特殊情况下生育二胎。但调查显示，很多夫妻迫于不断加重的经济压力，放弃生育二胎。因此，要从根本上解决老龄化的问题不能依靠出生率的提升，最有效的办法是建立有效的社会保障制度。

【参考译文】

Nowadays, China is stepping into the aging society. Therefore, the only child generation is facing enormous pressure both from work and life. The Chinese government has begun to adjust the family planning policy and allows some families to have a second child under certain circumstances. However, the survey shows that some couples give up the right to have a second child due to the increasing financial burden. Thus, in order to solve the aging problem, the basic thing is not to rely on the increase of birth rate. The best solution is to establish an effective social security system.

（引自 http://www.putclub.com/html/exam/cet6/2014/0418/85206.html）

【重点词汇】

小康社会　a well-off society
改革开放　reform and opening-up
公务员　civil servants
名人　celebrity
福利彩票　welfare lotteries
家政服务　household management service
民工　migrant laborers
职业道德　work ethics
应试教育　exam-oriented education
人口老龄化　aging of population
雾霾天气　hazy weather
环保产品　environment-friendly products
开发可再生资源　to develop renewable resources

可降解一次性塑料袋　　throwaway bio-degradable plastic bags

白色污染　　white pollution (by using and littering of non-degradable white plastics)

2. 经济发展

【例文 1】

中国特色互联网

全球互联网不仅没有使世界千人一面,反而被各种本土力量塑造得丰富多彩,中国互联网就是最佳佐证。中国用户的需求、中国企业家的态度、中国网下经济的发展以及政府扮演的角色正赋予其鲜明特色。因此,中国互联网规模不但日益壮大,而且其发展愈发具有中国特色。然而随着该行业与中国经济日益成熟,中国互联网还会继续保有这种鲜明特色吗？也许一些不同于西方的特色将会慢慢消失。而其他特色,如三大数字综合企业——阿里巴巴、百度与腾讯的主导之势,会保留下来。

【参考译文】

The Chinese Internet is the best example to illustrate that, far from creating uniformity, the global network is shaped by local forces. The demands of Chinese consumers, the attitudes of Chinese entrepreneurs, China's offline economic development and the role of the state are endowing it with distinctive features. Therefore China's Internet grows not only larger but also more distinctly Chinese. However, as the industry and China's economy mature, will China's Internet continue to have distinctively Chinese characteristics? Probably some differences from the West's will fade while other features will remain, for example the dominance of three digital conglomerates, Alibaba, Baidu and Tencent.

(引自 http://www.kekenet.com/Article/201108/146939.shtml)

【例文 2】

对外开放

中国将进一步发展经济、扩大开放,这对海外企业意味着更多的商机。改革开放以来,中国企业与海外企业一直积极开展经济技术合作,并取得了巨大成就。海外企业不仅帮助了中国企业的成长,而且也在合作中获得了收益。中国政府将继续提供有利的政策和条件,推动中国企业与国外企业进一步开展合作。

【参考译文】

China will develop its economy further and open itself wider to the outside world, which offers more business opportunities to overseas enterprises. Since

China's reform and opening up, Chinese enterprises have been cooperating with overseas enterprises in terms of economy and technology, and have scored great achievement. Overseas enterprises have not only helped Chinese enterprises with their growth, but also benefited from the cooperation. Chinese government will continue to offer favorable policies and conditions to promote the further cooperation between Chinese and overseas enterprises.

(参考"中华考试网":http://www.examw.com/cet4/trans/442958/)

【重点词汇】

第三产业　the tertiary sector of the economy
信息技术产业　IT
中外合资企业　joint ventures
国有企业　state-owned enterprises (SOEs)
私营企业　private businesses
民营企业　privately-run businesses
中小企业　small-and-medium-sized enterprises
金融　finance　　　　　　物流　logistics
制造　manufacture　　　　外包　outsource service
购买力　purchasing power　通货紧缩　deflation
通货膨胀　inflation　　　　经济繁荣　economic boom
经济萧条　economic depression

3. 城市介绍

【例文1】

上　海

上海位于中国东部,是中华人民共和国最大的城市。由于过去20年的迅猛发展,上海已再次成为国际化大都市,被称作"东方的巴黎"。上海有世界上最大的货物港口和全球最繁忙的海港,中国25%的工业总产值来自于这里的海上。上海为中国贡献了30%的GDP。截至2009年,有787家金融机构落户上海,其中170家为外资。如今,上海已再次成为世界最繁荣的城市之一。它的大都市气质、尖端富裕的消费者以及高学历的技术人才使它引起了海外投资者的关注。

【参考译文】

Shanghai, situated in East China, is the largest city of the People's Republic of China. Due to its rapid growth over the past two decades, it has again become a global city, also known as "the Paris in the East". Because of Shanghai's biggest port for cargo and the busiest sea port in the world, 25% of Chinese industrial output comes from the city on the sea. Moreover, Shanghai has produced 30% of

China's GDP. By the end of 2009, there are 787 financial institutions in Shanghai, of which 170 were foreign invested. Today, Shanghai is again one of the most prosperous cities in the world attracting investors overseas with its cosmopolitan characters, sophisticated affluent consumers and highly educated technical talents.

(参考"十分钟带你看懂上海"http://v.youku.com/v_show/id_XMzI5MzUxMTky.html)

【例文2】

苏　州

苏州是一个多水多桥、引人入胜的风光城市。它地处长江下游,气候温和,土地肥沃,再加上湖泊密布、水道纵横,自唐代以来就有"鱼米之乡"的美称。苏州是如此的美丽,很多人在这都是流连忘返。

Suzhou is a fascinating city of tourist attractions, dotted with bridges and waterways. Situated in the lower reaches of the Yangtze River and blessed with a mild climate, fertile soil, and numerous lakes and waterways across the region, it has enjoyed a reputation as "a land of milk and honey" ever since the Tang Dynasty. Suzhou is so beautiful that many people are reluctant to leave it.

(参考:许建平.研究生英语实用翻译教程[M].北京:中国人民大学出版社,2008.原文有修改。)

【重点词汇】

四季如春　It's like spring all the year round
四季分明　has four distinct seasons
冬暖夏凉　It is cool in summer and warm in winter
温暖湿润　warm and humid
河流上(中、下)游　in the upper (middle, lower) reaches of
南(北)岸　on the south (north) shore
河流贯穿　river runs through
沿海　along the coast; coastal
入海口　estuary, mouth
地势低平　low-lying
土地肥沃　fertile soil

课外练习

一、翻译理论

1. 翻译评析。

"山重水复疑无路,柳暗花明又一村。"出自南宋诗人陆游的《游山西村》。温家宝在中外记者招待会上引用了这句诗,由翻译张璐译为英语;美国国务卿希拉里到中国上海参加世博会时,也在其英文演讲中引用了这句诗。请比较以下两个翻译版本:

译文一:

There is a poem from the Southern Song Dynasty that reads:"After endless mountains and rivers that leave doubt whether there is a path out, suddenly one encounters the shade of a willow, bright flowers and a lovely village."

译文二:

After encountering all kinds of difficulties and experiencing all kinds of hardships, at the end of the day we will see light at the end of tunnel.

(1) 哪个版本是张璐的翻译,哪个出自希拉里的演讲?为什么?

(2) 哪个是直译,哪个是意译?

(3) 在哪个版本中用到了归化的翻译手法,这种归化处理有何根据?

2. 以下段落摘选自人物传记 *Steve Jobs*,请将其译为汉语。

Steve Jobs knew from an early age that he was adopted. "My parents were very open with me about that," he recalled. He had a vivid memory of sitting on the lawn of his house, when he was six or seven years old, telling the girl who lived across the street. "So does that mean your real parents didn't want you?" the girl asked. "Lightning bolts went off in my head," according to Jobs. "I remember running into the house, crying. And my parents said, 'No, you have to understand.' They were very serious and looked me straight in the eye. They said, 'We specifically picked you out.' Both of my parents said that and repeated it slowly for me. And they put an emphasis on every word in that sentence."

二、汉英语比较

以下汉语句子是《十分钟看懂中国》部分解说词的汉语译文,请写出它们的英文原文,注意比较二者的差异。

(1) 中华人民共和国,简称中国,位于东亚。

(2) 中国有 56 个民族,汉族人口占总人口的 92%。

(3) 中国是文明古国之一,有五千年文明,世袭的封建王朝终结于 1912 年。

(4) 中国古代有许多重要的科技发明,包括印刷术、造纸术、火药和指南针。也有很多著名的建筑,比如绵延四千英里的长城。

(5) 预测 2011 年到 2015 年,(中国)年均 GDP 增长会保持 9.5%。

(6) 中国是世界最大的出口国,第二大进口国,也是世界第二大奢侈品消费国。

(7) 汉语的方言很多,使用最多的是普通话和粤语。

(8) 门窗会贴上红色的剪纸和对联,象征幸福、富裕和长寿。

(9) 中国人喜欢红色,红色象征着繁荣和吉利。

(10) 每个地方都有自己的特色(食品),中国人也乐于向外人推荐。

(11) 中国的食物基本上都很健康并且摆放美观。

三、语体与翻译

1. 请判断以下词汇和结构中哪个语体层次更高,用">"或"<"表示。
例如:ascend 比 rise 语体层次更高,括号内填">"。ascend (>) rise。

(1) commence（　）begin.
(2) quit（　）resign; fatigued（　）tired; fail（　）flunk.
(3) put up with（　）tolerate; take part in（　）participate.
(4) I am（　）I'm; It is（　）it's.

2. 请判断下列各对句子中,哪个更正式,在更正式的那个句子后的括号里打勾。

(1) Revenue-raising proposal was also discussed to hike the fuel tax. （　）
Also discussed was a revenue-raising proposal to hike the fuel tax. （　）
(2) Since we live in the country, nobody visited us. （　）
Living in the country, we had few social visits. （　）
(3) Since the weather had improved, we decided to go swimming. （　）
The weather having improved, we decided to go swimming. （　）
(4) He tried to prevent the marriage but it took place all the same. （　）
He endeavored to prevent the marriage; however, they got married notwithstanding. （　）
(5) He left early so as not to miss the train. （　）
He left early in order that he would not miss the train. （　）
(6) Everybody looked after himself. （　）
Everybody looked after themselves. （　）

四、词义的确定和词性转换

1. 翻译下列句子,注意画线词语词义的选择,必要时进行引申。

(1) He halted in the district where by night are found the lightest street, hearts, vows(誓言) and librettos(歌曲). （根据语境和搭配确定词义）

(2) He managed to make a living with his pen. （抽象化引申）

(3) The country has the advantage of peace and quiet, but suffers the disadvantage of being cut off. （修辞性引申）

(4) 他万万没想到在他前进的路上竟然会出现这么多的拦路虎。（抽象化引申）

2. 翻译下列句子，注意英语名词和汉语动词之间的转换。
(1) He made no mention of his resignation.

(2) A look at his photos reminded me of our school days.

(3) The American airline industry has enjoyed significant expansion in the last twenty years.

(4) Lin Zexu believed that a successful ban of the trade in opium must be preceded by the destruction of the drug itself.

3. 翻译下列句子，注意英语形容词和汉语动词之间的转换。
(1) Crying is considered to be characteristic of woman.

(2) 谁负责这座大楼的保养事宜？

4. 翻译下列句子，注意英语介词与汉语动词之间的转换。
(1) The book is beyond my understanding.

(2) They are on their honeymoon abroad.

(3) 他<u>不戴眼镜</u>就跟瞎子一样。

(4) 他<u>不顾一切困难</u>坚持工作。

五、词的增减

1. 翻译下列句子,注意恰当增译。
(1) We won't retreat; we never have and never will.

(2) When she came to, she saw smiling faces around her.

(3) Before liberation, his mother lived on washing.

(4) 前途(prospects)一片光明,道路迂回曲折。

2. 翻译下列句子,注意恰当减译。
(1) 多年来那个国家一直有严重的失业现象。

(2) 人们利用科学去了解自然,改造自然。

(3) I was too tired to talk with you.

(4) He shrugged his shoulders, shook his head, closed his eyes, but said nothing.

3. 改译练习：

以下段落选自《乔布斯传》。背景：小学五年级的乔布斯成绩优异。老师让他跳级直接升到中学（六年级）。但是中学在一个治安混乱的社区，让他备受困扰。根据你学过的翻译技巧，该段的翻译还可以做哪些改进？

The transition was wrenching. He was a socially awkward loner who found himself with kids a year older. Worse yet, the sixth grade was in a different school, Crittenden Middle. It was only eight blocks from Monta Loma Elementary, but in many ways it was a world apart, located in a neighborhood filled with ethnic gangs. "Fights were a daily occurrence; as were shakedowns in bathrooms," wrote the Silicon Valley journalist Michael S. Malone. "Knives were regularly brought to school as a show of macho."

这样一种过渡有些突然。这个社交笨拙的孤独者发现自己身处一群比自己大一岁的人中间。更糟糕的是，他读六年级的地方是另一所学校。这所学校地处一个充斥着少数族裔帮派的社区，离原来的蒙塔洛马小学不过八条街之隔，但在很多方面却像另一个世界。"打架是每天发生的事，厕所里的敲诈也是如此，"硅谷记者迈克尔 S. 马隆这样写道，"学生们经常把刀带到学校来作为一种男子气概的展示。"

六、视角转换

1. 翻译下列句子，注意正反表达的准确、自然和贴切。

(1) We can't wait to meet you.

(2) Before I could protest, he got to his feet.

(3) I don't think he's qualified.

(4) Both sides thought that the peace proposal was one they could accept with dignity.

(5) In the absence of force, a body（物体）will either remain at rest or continue to move with constant speed in a straight line.

(6) The fact that some day nuclear energy will replace the energy from coal and oil cannot be overemphasized.

(7) Every person cannot become a great artist, and only the gifted and diligent can create brilliant artistic works that touch the softest part of a human heart.

(8) Certainly I don't teach because teaching is easy for me. Nor do I teach because I think I know answers, or because I have knowledge I feel compelled to share.

2. 翻译下列句子，注意被动语态的恰当处理。
(1) The compass was invented in China four thousand years ago.

(2) The credit system in America was first adopted by Harvard University in 1872.

(3) Our foreign policy is supported by the people all over the world.

(4) Measures have been taken to prevent the epidemic（流行病）from spreading quickly.

(5) It is often said that the joy of traveling is not in arriving at your destination but in the journey itself.

(6) Heat is constantly produced by the body as a result of muscular and cellular activity.

七、英语长句的翻译

1. 将下列句子译为汉语。

(1) It was a keen disappointment when I had to postpone the visit which I had intended to pay to U. S. in February.

(2) When I look down and see the prodigious fleet they have collected, I cannot help being astonished that a people should come 3000 miles at such risk, trouble and expense to rob, plunder and destroy another people because they will not lay their lives and fortune at their feet.

(3) Descendants of some of the 1500 people killed when the Titanic sank a century ago were among the passengers on a cruise ship that set off from Britain on Sunday to retrace the route of the liner's ill-fated voyage.

(4) A Southeast Airlines Boeing 737 carrying 142 people overshot the runway on landing at Burbank airport on Sunday, hitting a car with a woman and a child in it before coming to rest at the edge of a gas station, officials said.

(5) Human beings have distinguished themselves from other animals, and in doing so ensured their survival, by the ability to observe and understand their environment and then either to adapt to that environment or to control and adapt it to their own needs.

(6) Obama won re-election on Tuesday night despite a fierce challenge from Republican Mitt Romney, prevailing in the face of a weak economy and high unemployment that encumbered his first term and crimped the middle class dreams of millions.

2. 将下面一则新闻翻译成汉语。

Washington(**CNN**) The United States is delaying a long-planned missile test to avoid any misperceptions by North Korea amid mounting tensions, a senior U.S. Department of Defense official said Saturday.

Postponing the launch of the Minuteman Ⅲ intercontinental ballistic missile("民兵-3"洲际弹道导弹), initially scheduled for Tuesday at Vandenberg(范登堡) Air Force Base in California, was "prudent and wise", said the official, speaking on condition of anonymity.

The missile test had nothing to do with North Korea, but the United States decided to hold off "given recent tensions on the Korean Peninsula", the official said.

"The U.S. will conduct another test soon and remains strongly committed to our nuclear deterrence capabilities," said the official, who was not authorized to publicly release details of the launch.

八、定语从句的翻译

1. 将下面的句子翻译成汉语。

(1) Each team plays ten or eleven games each season which begins in September and ends in November.

(2) It is he who received the letter that announced the death of your uncle.

(3) She was very patient towards the children, which her husband seldom was.

(4) We know that a cat, whose eyes can take in many more rays than our eyes, can see clearly in the night.

(5) For any machine whose input and output forces are known, its mechanical advantage can be calculated.

(6) The meeting was postponed, which was exactly what we wanted.

(7) Behaviorists suggest that the child who is raised in an environment where there are many stimuli which develop his or her capacity for appropriate responses will experience greater intellectual development.

(8) Somebody tapped me on the shoulder and I looked up from the exercise books of my young pupils, which I was just correcting, into the lined, kind and smiling face of a little old woman.

2. 请将下面一则新闻译为汉语,注意其中定语从句的翻译。

《城管来了》:北京城管出书"正名"

An urban administrator in Beijing has been thrust into the spotlight after the release of his new bestselling book in which he openly discusses working in the city management system, China Youth Daily reports.

"Chengguan: an Insider's View" by Song Zhigang, a Beijing chengguan (urban administrator who is responsible for city management), tackles the role of chengguans in China, which has long been a major issue of contention because of their love-hate relationship with city residents. While their job duties include helping people and making the city better, they also must crack down on street vendors who operate without a license. While the chengguans receive smiles and thank-yous from local residents, they also are constantly showered in sarcasm for stripping people of their livelihoods and being inhumane and violent. In his book, Song shares his personal experiences as a chengguan and says he believes there are inadequacies in China's city management system. He expresses his opinion on the social problems that are common in Beijing and across China, which show no sign of abating despite all the efforts to solve them. "The current city management is far from satisfactory," he writes. "Chengguans are rude and violent, which makes both the residents and us unhappy. It just won't work. Our city should be more tolerant, more people-oriented and more beautiful."

九、汉译英：主语的选择

翻译下列句子，括号内给定的词供参考：
(1) 上海曾经发生过很多重大的历史事件。(witness)

(2) 墙壁和天花板使用了吸音材料。(sound absorbing material)

(3) 利用煤和石油可以制造各种各样有用的东西。

(4) 要创造新物质，就需要一个超热和高能的环境。

(5) 一想到要吻它我就恶心。(《青蛙王子》)(thought)

(6) 千里之堤，溃于蚁穴。

(7) 至今还不知道洛克比空难(the Lockerbie disaster)是哪个恐怖组织干的。

(8) 最易磨损的是鞋跟的外侧。

十、汉译英：谓语的处理和其他成分的安排

请用给定的词翻译下列汉语句子，注意主语、谓语的确定和从属成分的安排。
(1) 寒冷的天气已使所有的树叶都变黄了。
cold weather, turn, leaves, yellow

(2) 家家房顶上都装了供沐浴用的太阳能热水器。
roof, every house, solar heater, install, provide, warm water, shower

(3) 屈原怀着十分悲痛的心情，抱了一块石头，投汨罗江自杀了。
Qu Yuan, overwhelm, grief, drown himself, Miluo River, large stone, arms

(4) 他跳起来，连忙跑到盥洗室的镜子前，细看他脸上的伤口。
jump up, hasten to, mirror, bathroom, examine, cut, cheek

(5) 钱学森回国后，马上向政府呈交了一份报告，极力主张组建国防工业。
return, present, report, urge, establishment, national defense industry

(6) 美国的医疗体制在强大的市场推动下经历了一些深刻的自我变革。
American healthcare system, drive, powerful, market forces, undergo, profound, self-reform

十一、汉语长句的翻译

1. 将下列句子译为汉语，注意分句的合并。

(1) 小李是一位新生。他来自南方的一个省份。小李说一口方言，我们觉得很难听懂他说话。

(2) 上周五我去飞机场为一位老朋友送行,他应美国某州立大学的邀请,即将飞往该国讲学一年。

(3) 这个年轻人看起来很平常,竟有一所大房子,还有一辆豪车,这真让人难以置信。

2. 将下列短文译为英语。
(1) 对于一个在北平住惯的人,像我,冬天要是不刮风,便觉得是奇迹;济南的冬天是没有风声的。对于一个刚由伦敦回来的人,像我,冬天要能看得见日光,便觉得是怪事;济南的冬天是响晴的。自然,在热带的地方,日光是永远那么毒,响亮的天气,反有点叫人害怕。可是,在北中国的冬天,而能有温晴的天气,济南真的算个宝地。

(2) 端午节,又叫龙舟节,是为了纪念爱国诗人屈原。屈原是一位忠诚和受人敬仰的大臣,他给国家带来了和平和繁荣。但最后因为受到诽谤而最终投河自尽。人们撑船到他自尽的地方,抛下粽子,希望鱼儿吃粽子,不要吃屈原的身躯。几千年来,端午节的特色在于吃粽子和赛龙舟,尤其是在一些河湖密布的南方省份。

（3）即便当下的就业形势异常严峻,截至目前,大学文凭仍然是最好的长期投资。本周,布鲁金斯学会(Brookings Institution)发布的一项研究称,比起股票、债券、房产,甚至是黄金来说,大学文凭的回报率都要更高。无可否认,四年的大学本科学位要花费 102000 美元,两年的专科学位要花 28000 美元。确实是一大笔钱。但这项研究发现,从长期来看,这笔投入十分划算。

附 录

翻译考试与翻译竞赛

一、目前全国性的翻译考试

1. 全国外语翻译证书考试

全国外语翻译证书考试(National Accreditation Examinations for Translators and Interpreters,NAETI),是由教育部考试中心与北京外国语大学联合举办,在全国实施的面向全体公民的非学历证书考试。主要测试应试者的笔译和口译能力,并对应试者提供翻译资格的权威认证。该考试每年举行两次,分别安排在5月和11月。英语包括四个级别,即1~4级。各个级别均包括笔译和口译两种证书。

详情请参阅中国教育考试网:http://www.neea.edu.cn

全国外语翻译证书考试官网:http://sk.neea.edu.cn/wyfyzs/

2. 全国翻译专业资格(水平)考试

全国翻译专业资格(水平)考试(China Accreditation Test for Translators and Interpreters,CATTI)是受国家人力资源和社会保障部委托,由中国外文出版发行事业局负责实施与管理的一项国家级职业资格考试,是一项在全国实行的、统一的、面向全社会的翻译专业资格(水平)认证,是对参试人员口译或笔译方面双语互译能力和水平的评价与认定。

考试分7个语种——英、日、法、阿拉伯、俄、德、西班牙;四个等级——资深翻译和一至三级;两大类别——笔译、口译。口译又分交替传译和同声传译两个专业类别。该考试2003年12月开始,与翻译专业硕士学位教育实现接轨,每年两次:5月、11月。

华中科技大学设有口译考场,湖北省考试院设有笔译考场。

翻译专业资格(水平)考试官网:http://www.catti.net.cn/node_75061.htm

二、全国性翻译竞赛

1. 韩素音青年翻译奖竞赛

本竞赛由《中国翻译》杂志社主办,是目前中国翻译界组织时间最长、规模最大、影响最广的翻译大赛,1986年开始,每年一届。

中国译协网:www.tac-online.org.cn

2. 新纪元全球华文青年文学奖(含翻译奖)

由香港中文大学文学院主办,2005年开始,每年一届。

http://www.literary.arts.cuhk.edu.hk

3. "CASIO杯"翻译竞赛

由上海市文学艺术界联合会、上海世纪出版股份有限公司主办,上海翻译家协会、上海译文出版社《外国文艺·译文》杂志社承办,卡西欧(上海)贸易有限公司协办,2004年开始,每年一届。

上海译文出版社:www.yiwen.com.cn

上海翻译家协会:www.sta.org.cn

卡西欧:www.casio.com.cn/dic

4. "优萌杯"翻译竞赛

由复旦大学外文学院主办,2006年开始,每年一届。

复旦大学外文学院:http://dfll.fudan.edu.cn

外语教学与研究出版社:http://www.fltrp.com

高等英语教学网:http://www.heep.cn

5. "语言桥杯"翻译大赛

由四川外语学院研究生部主办,是西南地区唯一的全国性翻译大赛。2003年开始,每年一届。

四川外语学院:http://www.sisu.edu.cn

重庆语言桥翻译有限公司:http://www.lan-bridge.com

6. "《英语世界》杯"翻译大赛

始于2010年,由商务印书馆《英语世界》杂志社主办。

商务印书馆:http://www.cp.com.cn

《英语世界》官方博客:http://blog.sia.com.cn/theworldofenglish

7. "语言桥杯"全国高校笔译邀请赛

主办单位:西安外国语大学、西安语言桥语言信息技术有限公司、环球网。

承办单位:西安外国语大学高级翻译学院,始于2012年,每年一届。

比赛网址:http://218.30.67.26:9000/

8. "芙蓉杯"青年翻译奖

2006年开始,中南大学外国语学院和《外语与翻译》编辑部主办。

邮寄地址为长沙市韶山南路22号中南大学铁道校区《外语与翻译》编辑部,邮编为410075。

中南大学外国语学院:http://sfl.csu.edu.cn

主要参考文献和网站

[1] Halliday M A K, Hasan R. Cohesion in English [M]. London:Longman, 1976.
[2] Halliday M A K. An Introduction to Functional Grammar [M]. London: Edward Arnold, 1985.
[3] Newmark, P. A Textbook of Translation[M]. 上海:上海外语教育出版社, 2001.
[4] Eugene A Nida. Translating meaning [M]. California:English Language Institute, 1982.
[5] Eugene A Nida. On Translation [M]. Beijing:China Translation & Publishing Corporation,1984.
[6] Eugene A Nida, Taber R Charles. The Theory and Practice of Translation [M]. Leiden:E. J. Brill, 1969.
[7] Alexander F Tyler. Essay on the principles of Translation [M]. Amsterdam: John Benjamins, 1978.
[8] Howard Goldblatt. Life and Death Are Wearing Me out [M]. New York: Arcade Publishing, Inc. ,2006.
[9] Mark Shuttleworth, Moira Cowie. Dictionary of Translation Studies [M]. Manchester:St. Jerome, 1997.
[10] Walter Isaacson. Steve Jobs[M]. New York:Simon & Schuster, 2011.
[11] 蔡基刚. 英汉写作对比研究 [M]. 上海:复旦大学出版社,2001.
[12] 曹明伦. 广告语言的基本特点及其翻译[J]. 中国翻译, 2006,27(6):87-89.
[13] 陈安玲. 认知视角对语篇语域的设定[J]. 外国语言文学, 2007,(1):20-23.
[14] 陈宏薇. 汉英翻译基础[M]. 上海:上海外语教育出版社, 1997.
[15] 陈宏薇,李亚丹.新编汉英翻译教程[M]. 上海:上海外语教育出版社, 2004.
[16] 陈宏薇. 新实用汉译英教程 [M].武汉:湖北教育出版社,1995.
[17] 陈玉. 电影字幕翻译中功能对等理论应用分析——以电影《冰河世纪3》字幕翻译为例[J]. 哈尔滨学院学报,2012,33(7):68-71.
[18] 邓跃平. 翻译教学的事件分析途径——定语从句的翻译[J]. 中国科技翻译, 2011,24(3):35-38.

[19] 段义涛. 中国文化英语 80 主题[M]. 北京:中国宇航出版社,2010.
[20] 方梦之. 英汉翻译基础教程[M]. 北京:中国对外翻译出版有限公司,2005.
[21] 郭奕奕. 汉译英中主语的选择[J]. 上海科技翻译,2000,(5):28-29.
[22] 黄湘. 科技英语无灵名词作主语汉译种种[J]. 中国科技翻译,1997,10(4):16-22.
[23] 丁衡祁. 翻译广告文字的立体思维[J]. 中国翻译,2004,25(1):75-80.
[24] 冯庆华. 实用翻译教程[M]. 上海:上海外语教育出版社,2008.
[25] 范仲英. 实用翻译教程[M]. 北京:外语教学与研究出版社,1997.
[26] 管新平,何志平. 汉英等效翻译[M]. 广州:华南理工大学出版社,2006.
[27] 何刚强. 笔译理论与技巧[M]. 北京:外语教学与研究出版社,2009.
[28] 侯维瑞. 英语语体[M]. 上海:上海外语教育出版社,1988.
[29] 柯平. 英汉与汉英翻译教程[M]. 北京:北京大学出版社,1990.
[30] 李丙午,燕静敏. 科技英语的名词化结构及其翻译[J]. 中国科技翻译,2002,15(1):5-7.
[31] 李怀先. 科技英语汉译琐谈[J]. 中国科技翻译,1988,(1):26-32.
[32] 李克新. 论广告翻译的策略[J]. 中国翻译,2004,25(6):64-69.
[33] 李萍. 中国文化背景[M]. 北京:世界图书出版公司,1998.
[34] 李学平. 通过翻译学英语[M]. 天津:南开大学出版社,2011.
[35] 李亚丹. 英译汉名篇赏析[M]. 武汉:湖北教育出版社,1999.
[36] 刘宓庆. 翻译基础[M]. 上海:华东师范大学出版社,2008.
[37] 刘宓庆. 新编汉英对比与翻译[M]. 北京:中国对外翻译出版有限公司,2006.
[38] 刘宓庆. 汉英对比研究与翻译[M]. 江西:江西教育出版社,1991.
[39] 刘宓庆. 文体与翻译[M]. 北京:中国对外翻译出版有限公司,1998.
[40] 刘明东. 英语被动语态的语用分析及其翻译[J]. 中国科技翻译,2001,14(1):1-4.
[41] 刘文俊. 科技英语翻译也讲究"雅"[J]. 中国科技翻译,1994,(3):9-15.
[42] 骆海辉. 省略法在汉英翻译中的应用[J]. 美中外语,2005,3(3):59-62.
[43] 吕和发,单丽平. 汉英公示语词典[M]. 北京:商务印书馆,2009.
[44] 毛荣贵. 新世纪大学英汉翻译教程[M]. 上海:上海交通大学出版社,2002.
[45] 潘福燕. 英语科技文体的语词特点及翻译[J]. 中国科技翻译,2005,18(4):56-58.
[46] 潘文国. 公共场所英语标志语错译解析与规范[M]. 上海:上海外语教育出版社,2010.
[47] 秦秀白. 英语语体和文体要略[M]. 上海:上海外语教育出版社,2002.
[48] 宋德富,张美兰. 英汉公示语即查即用手册[M]. 北京:中国水利水电出版社,

2010.
- [49] 宋洪波. 大学英语 6 级模拟试题[M]. 上海:上海外语教育出版社,2013.
- [50] 苏吉儒,陈敏. 科技翻译中的准确性刍议[J]. 中国科技翻译,1994,7(1):16-18.
- [51] 孙致礼. 中国的文学翻译:从归化趋向异化[J]. 中国翻译,2002,23(1):40-44.
- [52] 孙致礼. 新编英汉翻译教程[M]. 上海:上海外语教育出版社,2003.
- [53] 谭卫国. 英汉广告修辞的翻译[J]. 中国翻译,2003,24(2):62-65.
- [54] 谭载喜. 奈达论翻译[M]. 北京:中国对外翻译出版有限公司,1984.
- [55] 魏志成,余军. 汉英比较翻译教程练习[M]. 北京:清华大学出版社,2006.
- [56] 王春晖. 科技英语否定结构的翻译[J]. 中国科技翻译,1989,2(3):17-23.
- [57] 王大伟. 现代汉英翻译技巧[M]. 北京:世界图书出版公司,1999.
- [58] 王大伟. 英语笔译实务 3 级教材配套训练[M]. 北京:外文出版社,2010.
- [59] 王鸣阳. 科技翻译中的直译倾向——兼谈科技翻译的任务[J]. 中国科技翻译,1988,(1):18-20.
- [60] 王泉水. 科技英语定语从句的非定语化译法[J]. 中国科技翻译,1999,12(1):15.
- [61] 王卫平. 英汉互译——方法与实践[M]. 武汉:华中科技大学出版社,2007.
- [62] 王卫平,潘丽蓉. 英语科技文献的语言特点与翻译[M]. 上海:上海交通大学出版社,2009.
- [63] 王治奎. 大学英汉翻译教程[M]. 济南:山东大学出版社,2004.
- [64] 辛凌,王婷. 大学英语实用翻译教程[M]. 重庆:重庆大学出版社,2009.
- [65] 许建平. 研究生英语实用翻译教程[M]. 北京:中国人民大学出版社,2008.
- [66] 许建平. 英汉互译——实践与技巧[M]. 北京:清华大学出版社,2003.
- [67] 许建平. 大学英语实用翻译[M]. 北京:中国人民大学出版社,2009.
- [68] 阎庆甲. 科技英语翻译手册[M]. 郑州:河南科学技术出版社,1986.
- [69] 闫文培. 实用科技英语翻译要义[M]. 北京:科学出版社,2008.
- [70] 杨莉藜. 英汉互译教程[M]. 开封:河南大学出版社,1996.
- [71] 杨静怡. 论汉译英过程中视角转换的作用[J]. 漳州师范学院学报,2008,(2):110-113.
- [72] 杨寿康. 论科技英语与科技翻译[M]. 合肥:安徽文艺出版社,2003.
- [73] 杨树达. 汉文文言修辞学[M]. 北京:中华书局,1980.
- [74] 杨文秀. 科技英语翻译读本[M]. 南京:南京大学出版社,2012.
- [75] 管延圻,魏群,余倩,等. 史蒂夫·乔布斯传[M]. 北京:中信出版社,2011.
- [76] 廖月娟,姜雪影,谢凯蒂. 贾伯斯传[M]. 台北:天下远见出版有限公司,2011.
- [77] 殷燕. 试析电影字幕翻译策略[J]. 电影文学,2013,(12):156-157.

[78] 游长松,谢灵敏. 大学英语四级考试短文听写+段落翻译[M]. 上海:上海外语教育出版社,2013.

[79] 曾诚. 实用汉英翻译教程[M]. 北京:外语教学与研究出版社,2002.

[80] 张春柏. 英语笔译实务 3 级[M]. 北京:外文出版社,2011.

[81] 张春柏. 英汉汉英翻译教程[M]. 北京:高等教育出版社,2003.

[82] 张培基. 英汉翻译教程[M]. 上海:上海外语教育出版社,1980.

[83] 张群.《让子弹飞》英文字幕翻译中的互文策略[J]. 电影文学,2012,(15):158-159.

[84] 赵萱,郑仰成. 科技英语翻译[M]. 北京:外语教学与研究出版社,2006.

[85] 周志培. 汉英对比与翻译中的转换[M]. 上海:华东理工大学出版社,2003.

[86] 庄绎传. 英汉翻译简明教程[M]. 北京:外语教学与研究出版社,2002.

[87] 张梅岗. 限制性定语从句传统译法的探讨[J]. 中国翻译,2000,(5):23-26.

[88] 朱兰珍. 文化全球化语境下的文学翻译策略[J]. 作家杂志,2012,(5):187-188.

[89] 华中科技大学外国语学院《英汉互译》精品课程网站

[90] http://v.youku.com/v_show/id_XMzMyODkwNjQ0.html

[91] http://sti.blcu.edu.cn/bbs/showtopic-353.aspx

[92] http://www.wendu.com/sifa/149891.html

[93] http://wenku.baidu.com/view/2bc1c669011ca300a6c390f0.html

[94] http://www.kekenet.com/video/200903/65031.shtml

[95] www.elanso.com

[96] http://www.yywzb.com.cn/more.asp?infoid=1722

[97] http://www.douban.com/group/topic/4517131/

[98] http://v.youku.com/v_show/id_XMzI5MzUxMTky.html

[99] http://www.kekenet.com/Article/201108/146939.shtml

[100] http://www.putclub.com/html/exam/cet6/2014/0418/85206.html

[101] http://www.fane.cn/?p=2027445

[102] http://www.docin.com/p-210868722.html

[103] http://www.360doc.cn/article/99504_234072297.html

[104] http://www.docin.com/p-456862042.html

[105] http://www.examw.com/cet4/trans/442958/

[106] http://www.doc88.com/p-9982983029029.html

[107] http://www.examw.com/cet4/trans/438384/

[108] http://www.chinaqking.com/%D4%AD%B4%B4%D7%F7%C6%B7/2009/27711.html

[109] http://www.doc88.com/p-2902073544552.html